PSYCH2GO PRESENTS

THE PSYCHOLOGY
OF PEOPLE

PSYCH2GO PRESENTS

THE PSYCHOLOGY OF PEOPLE

A LITTLE BOOK OF PSYCHOLOGY & WHAT MAKES YOU YOU

BY PSYCH2GO & THOMAS KANG

mango
PUBLISHING GROUP

CORAL GABLES

Cover Design: Megan Werner
Cover Photo/illustration: Thomas Kang
Layout & Design: Megan Werner

For permission requests, please contact the publisher at:
Mango Publishing Group
2850 S Douglas Road, 2nd Floor
Coral Gables, FL 33134 USA
info@mango.bz

For special orders, quantity sales, course adoptions and corporate sales, please email the publisher at sales@mango.bz. For trade and wholesale sales, please contact Ingram Publisher Services at customer.service@ingramcontent.com or +1.800.509.4887.

Psych2Go Presents the Psychology of People: The Little Book of Psychology & What Makes You You

Library of Congress Cataloging-in-Publication number: 2023935069
ISBN: (pb) 978-1-68481-231-8 (hc) 978-1-68481-319-3 (e) 978-1-68481-232-5
BISAC category code: PSY020000, PSYCHOLOGY / Neuropsychology

Printed in the United States of America

TABLE OF CONTENTS

INTRODUCTION STUFF!

ABOUT US

Oh—apologies for the abrupt intro. We'd like to tell you more about who we are and what we do! And I mean we'd *really* like to let you know. Because it's overwhelmingly common for people to get the most engaged when they talk about themselves. There's your first cool psych fact of the book! Yay! (We promise, they get way cooler than that.) But anyways, who we are is simple—we're Psych2Go—a mental health informer aiming to spread interest and awareness in various topics within the psychology and wellness sphere using academic studies, expert opinions, and of course, our little buddy/ mascot Psi.

Say "Hi," Psi!

We believe in research-backed, practical advice and knowledge that serves to educate and comfort. With a following of more than ten million subscribers on YouTube and over 800,000 combined followers on other social media such as Instagram and Facebook, as well as a magazine, online blog, and interviewing presence, Psych2Go has firmly established itself as one of the front-runners in the business of making the machinations of the mind a marvel for the masses. Ahem. If we do say so ourselves.

I mean, that's cool and all I guess; mental health, education, ten million subscribers... But what does it all exactly...mean? These days, "mental health informer" is as broad a term as "operational assistant" or "big fan"—there's no indicator of the breadth, depth, or motivation behind the phrase. In the day and age of people constantly trying to one-up each other on their moral superiority, the proclamation that one is or should be a "mental health advocate" seems almost like a platitude. But believe us—we realize how grave this work is. We realize how devastating it is to be unwell and how all-consuming the void can be. That's not to make the presumptuous claim that we viscerally know exactly how heavy *your* burden is, or anyone else's for that matter—we're saying we know that in any case, it's present, it's real, and...it hurts. Sometimes it hurts just you, sometimes it hurts your family; sometimes it hurts your partner, sometimes it hurts everyone and anyone around you.

So why make a YouTube channel? Why run an internet presence at all?

Why write a book?

Simple—we have a mission. And that mission is to spread our message everywhere we can, especially in places where the ones who believe in it are most restricted. By being as present in as many places as possible, we can let people know that not only are they being heard by us, but we also want them to know it will be okay. And the more media through which we can achieve that, the better! Some fantastic stories, studies, and experiences out there will resonate better through pages in a book than frames in a video. We'll get you to master your mind and become aware of what's going on in others'—and we'll start by doing it with *science*!

WHAT SCIENCE?

You know, the discoveries and observations that we've made throughout history. We'll be discussing mostly the ones written down in a lab environment, as those are the most reliable and distilled descriptions and the science-y people we'll talk about tended to focus mostly on practical inquiry—i.e., stuff that you, lovely reader, would actually care about. We'd hope, though, that you're already interested in all of this! After all, it's safe to say that most people can agree that psychology is awesome. Seriously, who hasn't dreamed of gaining Professor X-like powers and taking over the world by reading the minds of all of your adversaries to gain a leg up on them? Just us? Is Professor X a dated reference now? He's the bald guy who reads minds. We'd estimate that this kind of superpower fantasy is at least, like, 65 percent relevant to psychology. After all, isn't psychology, like, a bunch of scientists trying to see what's going on in people's minds?

Honestly? Not that far off. Unlike in comic books, we in the real world can't just *nyoom* our way into other people's brains. What we do have, though, are estimations of how they kind of operate. You'll learn more about this later, but researchers have likened the facilities of the brain to how a computer works—a computer that we can analyze structurally (i.e., looking at the parts of the brain that you can theoretically touch and what they do) and behaviorally (i.e., what output do we get from a given input?). The inferences we make from these analyses give us hints about what underlies thoughts, feelings, and motivations.

If we want insights into why or how people react or feel about certain things, we run experiments. Lucky for us, experiments are conducted under a specific set of conditions that make it such that, for people like us, once the results are in, you have a decent understanding of the phenomenon it was looking at. Take that explanation with a grain of salt—a lot of other stuff muddies the water when it comes to these investigations. You know, stuff like the peer-review process and the politics of publishing and the selection bias of studies that get approved for funding in the first place and the inherently biased nature of certain analyses and the importance of context and confounding factors and... Well, we'll keep it simple—our presentation will already have these things factored in, so all you need to know is that this is generally what happens.

The body of cumulative knowledge gained through these studies is what we call "science"! Or more specifically, when referring to science that talks about human thoughts, feelings, and behaviors: "psychology"!

WHY READ ABOUT PSYCHOLOGY?

If there's anything that will enhance the reading experience of this book, it's learning *why* you're reading it. And that is what this section aims to assist with! If you're willing to graciously lend your time to read on for the next little bit in this section, it'll surely be worth it. Now, this isn't to say that flipping open a book for some leisure reading always has to be such a serious undertaking (like, can't my reason be that I'm bored?)—just that books are usually better enjoyed with a little sprinkle of context, is all.

Of course, if you've already made up your mind about the book, whatever your motivation, then good on you. It's important to note, though, that to a degree, everyone's reason for reading will be multifaceted. Even if you find yourself already set on reading, this introduction aims to introduce you to further virtues of a more sophisticated knowledge of psychology. We're trying to cover most of our bases here.

Some might be seeking a nice, light read that they can flip open at any time to chew on the trivia or ideas presented within. Others may find themselves drawn to this book for the potential to extract benign social manipulation tactics—or, as we call them nowadays, "psychological life hacks." Rest assured; you'll find your trivia and life hacks within the juicy, juicy pages of this book. But you want to know what this book is *really* all about? The whole reason it was written in the first place?

Well, it's about...*you*.

Yes, you. Did you become viscerally aware of your position in space just now? Does it suddenly feel like your vision has expanded past the periphery of this book's pages? Maybe you feel a little itch on your body that you didn't realize you were ignoring. Or maybe you realized your posture is out of whack. That's okay because, full disclosure, we were totally trying to spook you just now.

To get back to the matter at hand, we at Psych2Go know that to master psychology is to master oneself. To make an analogy, we'll say living life as You, the human, is like driving a car. Generally, as time goes on, most people become decently functional drivers (except that guy that cut me off yesterday; that was seriously rude)—you generally don't have to know the exact mechanisms of a car to pilot it; you learn and get better by driving more and accumulating experience. However, if you encounter a problem with your car, or get curious as to how it works, well...you won't know what everything under the hood does just by taking a cursory glance at it, no matter how many miles you have logged. Yes, the lived experience is vital, but so is obtaining the knowledge necessary to know what you're working with. This is why car manuals, mechanic apprenticeships, and online tutorials exist— because there are some things that you can't know intuitively or would at least be way too time-consuming or inefficient to find out yourself. Allow this book to be the manual for the human brain—specifically, *your* human brain!

What exactly is in it for us to talk about you, though? That is, talking about you, *to you*. Well, we believe that such knowledge could very well be one of the greatest tools we have in the fight against the mental health crisis which, at the time of writing, affects more than 50 percent of the world's population. **Stoicism** is a philosophical practice that attempts to ground itself emotionally by viewing the world as a set of facts and systems. If we can understand *why* we feel or think the things we do, maybe we can understand how to deal with those feelings and thoughts. To attain insight into the workings of the brain, despite its elusive nature, is to gain valuable perspective on life itself. The perspective of the objective world, free from speculatory bias. By no means is this a comprehensive summary of such a storied school of thought, but any more would be delving into territory beyond this book's purview.

"STEEL YOUR SENSIBILITIES, SO THAT LIFE SHALL HURT YOU AS LITTLE AS POSSIBLE."

—ZENO OF CITIUM

Of course, dissemination of clinical psychology facts isn't the only measure being taken for mental health advocacy—far from it. And just as well—it's possible that you aren't that concerned about this whole ordeal. Maybe you picked up this book because you want to sit down with some quirky trivia. That's completely valid; don't get us wrong. By putting this out there, we can at least say we've achieved one more instance of raising awareness for the issue.

In any case, we won't bog you down with any more of that deep, Socrates-type, "know thyself" mumbo. Whether or not you do care about all that stuff (it'd be nice if you did though!)—we hope you enjoy the book for some reason or another. It'll be useful for *something*, that's for sure. For example, did you feel more compelled to keep reading after we started this section with the sentence, "apologies for the abrupt intro"? If you felt just a little more convinced, you've experienced a psychology trick firsthand! There's more on that specific trick in its own dedicated section later, so keep reading. Or just flip to that section. We honestly don't mind. Really! The whole book is formatted so you can flip to any page and it'll still be fun to read.

CHAPTER 1

DO YOU SEE WHAT I SEE?

NEUROPSYCHOLOGY AND PERCEPTION

Back in ye olde days, our understanding of everything was kind of more nebulous. Illnesses were caused by bad vibes and miasma. Rain was water that spawned from space. There was less scientific method to it all and more intuiting about how things worked. That isn't to say these theories or models of the world were primitive; they laid the groundwork for the more empirical knowledge structures that we have today.

Well then, with that knowledge in mind, it won't be too much of a shocker that at one point we didn't have a framework within which we could think about how the human mind operates. To this day, the mind is this wishy-washy, abstract concept to most. Loads of people don't think of it as something that can even be analyzed using hard science. Providing context on how the smart science-type people have attempted to turn it into a true-blue scientific discipline will aid greatly in understanding what's coming up in this book. Though this knowledge is not necessary, it'll enhance your enjoyment and comprehension of the book! I think.

You probably have interacted with a computer at least once in your life. Right? Like, in any capacity—the computer in your phone (do you have a phone?), the computer in your car's GPS (do you have a car?), the computer in your robot dog's cranial casing (???)—

most people know their way around some sort of computational device. Let's take the basic example of a calculator—you put in numbers, tell it what operation you want performed, and get new numbers. That's crazy.

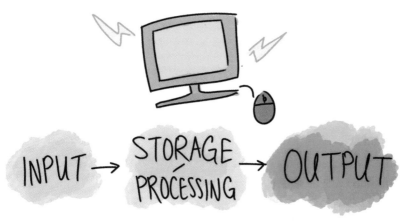

As we mentioned in the intro, this is how neuroscientists model the way our brains work. As computers. That is, input moves to storage/processing which moves to output. This might seem a little rudimentary, but it's taken a long time to reach that conclusion.

Since we all live in the same world, that would mean that the "input" for most people experiencing the same event would be the same. That also means that after processing, the "output" would yield the same thing—right? But that would mean a world where everyone reacts the same way as their friend or neighbor, and we know that that is definitely not the case. So, what gives?

First, the brain is way more complex than this simple model we've got here. You can truncate the process down to a few words, but we're taking each step for granted if we look at things superficially.

Let's begin with the "input" part; even when two people look at the same thing, they may not perceive it the same way. For instance, if you and Psi come from different cultures and observe a party full of people, you may recognize your friends, enjoy hearing your favorite song played on the speakers, and feel excited hearing people cheer in your native language. In contrast, Psi may see a group of unfamiliar faces, feel anxious about the DJ's turntable plugged into a loose outlet (that's a fire hazard!), and find everyone speaking in a foreign language they don't understand. You might take in the great scents of the sweet perfume of guests trying to impress each other, whereas Psi could be less sensitive to the smell of perfume and instead notice the odor of sweaty dancers on the dance floor. Although you are receiving the same visual, auditory, and olfactory inputs, you may be taking in a grand old time while Psi is taking in an anxiety attack waiting to happen.

And second, we're also skipping over the "processing" part a bit too haphazardly—many forces are at play regarding how we react to things (even if we don't realize we're reacting at all).

Our instinctual responses to past and present input can inform how we store and process future input. Someone compliments your clothes. You store it in your short-term memory so you don't immediately forget what they said. You have an internal reaction to the compliment (consisting of becoming a little bit happier) and an external reaction (consisting of a smile and a "thank you"). Now imagine this keeps happening. People often compliment your clothes whenever you show up to school (or work, or the olde-timey confectionery shoppe, etc.). Over many years, you have many fond memories of people complimenting you. From this, you gain lots of pride in your fashion sense. You carry yourself confidently whenever you wear a new outfit and are happy when thinking about clothes.

It's like you've been programmed to have a positive affinity for fashion and your appearance. This is evident in that we can feasibly imagine that someone could dress the same way as you but feel terrible about their appearance if they've only received negative feedback about their outfits.

You'll often find that when we experience something, we don't understand it by itself—we understand it in the context of what we know about everything around it.

For example, people tasting a new food for the first time will often say something like, "It tastes like this other food, except sweeter"—they're putting the perception of the flavor in the context of previous experiences. So if people are always contextualizing their situations, why do people sometimes act irrationally or feel things they "shouldn't"? Can't we ask people why they do the things they do, and they'll tell us the root cause? After all, they're the ones mapping out the context for themselves.

Well, what if the answer is...they don't know?

Psychologists in the early 1900s and many philosophical movements such as Buddhism converged on the idea that you don't actively have to think of something for it to affect you.

We take the idea for granted nowadays but early psychologists such as William James, Pierre Janet, and Sigmund Freud were some of the first and most famous ones to posit a system of thought influenced by things that weren't memories or knowledge being actively recalled. You don't always know why you dream about the things you do, but they couldn't have come from nowhere, right? This was the beginning of realizing we are heavily influenced by our subconscious. They got a lot of things wrong, of course, but those things could be ironed out later—the fact is, they got this banger of an idea correct: things that get lodged into our minds have a tight grip on how we think and react to things, whether we know it or not. Our brains sometimes control us, and not the other way around.

Maybe the reason you lashed out at your friend was because you had some leftover stress from being yelled at earlier today.

To bring this back to the computer analogy, we are unaware of what is inputted—and we're certainly unaware of how the storage and processing are corrupted, twisted, manipulated, and reinterpreted based on what went in and what's already there. We don't think a thought because we "decide on it"—it's more like thoughts happen *at* us. You don't see a jump scare in a scary movie and think, "Ah yes—quite scary! I've analyzed this situation, and this checks all the boxes for what I consider 'scary.' I should express this somehow!" and then make the conscious decision to scream and maybe pee a little. Your body decides to react first based on the framework it has in place to deal with the category of "scary things." Notably, this happens before you can even think about it. You can consciously try to brace yourself for a scary situation and make a concerted effort *not* to scream or pee, but you can see the voluntary part of the response is in the restraint of output and not the production of it.

The long and short of it is, our brains are gigantic, entangled spaghetti nests of frameworks intertwined with other frameworks built upon millions of years of evolution and cultural influences. An unbelievable amount of trial and error has brought us to the point that our thought and perception processes are highly efficient but only efficient enough to ensure our propagation as a species. You might think that your mind is working as well as it possibly can, that the world and how you think about it is how it appears. The fact of the matter is, however, that there's so much happening in the dark, unbeknownst to the most perceptive and objective individuals. In the end, there is a high degree to which we're subordinate to our programming. But are we to acquiesce to this fate? Or can we rise above our proverbial ones and zeroes to achieve an understanding of the world in a more holistic sense? Well, maybe we can start by learning the ins and outs of the pathways our inputs and processes take before becoming outputs.

SEEING THE WORLD IN LOW RESOLUTION

"Is a pile of several mashed potatoes just one gigantic mashed potato?"

Do you know what a thumbnail is? In the internet business, it's the little picture that represents the thing you're about to click. You know when you look up a video and next to the title is an image of the video, kind of like a book cover? That image is called a "thumbnail." It's not nearly as big as the video in content or image quality, but you can generally make out what it is and what it's trying to say most of the time if it's a good thumbnail.

You don't need the thumbnail to tell every detail of what will happen in the video because that's what the video is for—the thumbnail provides a good preview or summary of what you may be getting into if you click onward. Again, you can think of it kind of like a book cover—a cover won't have the entire text of the book written out on it—it's something to visually represent the book that you don't have to squint at to take in all the details.

INTRODUCTION TO HEURISTICS

Our mind works by packaging everything into tiny thumbnails. We call these heuristics. I won't do this often with new words, but I'd like you to remember to recognize this word going forward in this section. A heuristic is a shortcut. A cognitive heuristic, like a mental shortcut, is an attempt to bypass the complicated, detailed thinking process and apply a quick fix to whatever input you've just been faced with.

Let's take the example of stereotypes. Stereotypes are a common heuristic. The stereotypical clown, for example, has a set of traits associated with them automatically by their membership in the category of "clown." You'd probably think they're generally goofy, funny, skilled at making balloon animals, and nice to children. We use a heuristic—a shortcut—to assume some things about most clowns we meet so we don't have to interview them about their every trait and feel like we have to get to know them deeply and intimately to conclude who they are. Imagine sitting down for a chat with a clown and the first thing you ask is, "Are you funny?"—the idea of doing this seems silly because being funny is assumed from the outset.

The world would be a horrifying place to live if we didn't use heuristics. You probably don't realize when you're using them. We simplify everything, literally everything, that we see all the time. When you look at a person, you don't count every pore on their face, the exact stitching of the fabric of their clothes, and whether their socks are pulled up to symmetric heights. When you're in a room, you may not notice the presence of one or two items within it if they're not immediately in need of attention—this could include entire people. Speaking of not noticing other humans, think about when you see a crowd—you don't see individual faces; you see a blob of people. It's not that you're willfully ignoring them—it's more like the default state is ignorance and you have to make an effort to pay attention.

You might be thinking, "Wow, so much information is lost due to our use of heuristics. I have to learn to break free of using shortcuts and always be hyper-aware of my surroundings"—but this is not exactly, entirely, 100 percent, completely, undeniably true. Heuristics are so prevalent because they're really effective. Ninety times out of a hundred, they work just fine and present you with a serviceable picture of the world. The thumbnail isn't in 4K cinema quality, sure, but it's still legible enough for you to comfortably recognize the important bits. If your mind kept tabs of every single detail of every single *thing* around you at all times, you'd go insane in no time flat.

A practical application of heuristics that you've seen before but probably weren't aware of is in the Gestalt Principles of Perception. I'm not gonna lie, when I first heard about this, I thought "Gestalt" was the name of the person who made up this idea. But it's not a person—it's the German word approximating what we know in English as "shape" or "configuration." The idea was developed by Max Wertheimer, Kurt Koffka, and Wolfgang Köhler way back when (early 1900s-ish) so it should be called the Wertheimer-Koffka-Köhler Principles of Perception. Though this alternative name is largely impractical in common parlance, I like it because it is extremely intimidating and extremely German.

Before I explain what the Gestalt Principles, or gestaltism, is, why don't we see it in action using you, lovely reader, as the test subject?

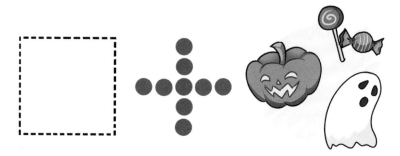

What are these depicting? Well, if you had to venture a guess, you'd probably say (in order):

- A square

- A cross

- Halloween

Now you can be pedantic about it and say, "Well, actually, it's a bunch of dotted lines arranged quadrilaterally, a collection of dots, and several icons evocative of Halloween celebrations"—yeah, okay. That's like, what they're made of. But you don't look at a cake and go, "Ah yes, flour and eggs!"—you call it a cake.

Back to the point: it's a square, a cross, and Halloween. And why can we reach those conclusions? You know, even though the outline of the square isn't complete, the cross is incidentally the shape made by the arrangement of the dots, and there's nothing around the Halloween symbols that explicitly states these things are present on October 31? This is another case of heuristics applied to our visual understanding of the world.

THE GESTALT PRINCIPLES OF PERCEPTION

The Gestalt Principles, or gestaltism, dictate that people see things as a whole. Our minds fill in blanks—if there's 70 percent of a picture of a square present, we can assume what is in front of us is, for all intents and purposes, a square. But wait, didn't I say this has a practical application? Well, other than using this to freak out your friends with optical illusions, it doesn't look like it. However, gestaltism informs an important and ubiquitous school of thought. Often people point to graphic design as a prime example of gestaltism's practical use case, but you can also apply it more broadly to things like music. Individual notes don't carry too much meaning behind them, but being played at the same time as another note to make a chord can communicate a mood immediately. You can even see this being applied in conversation—someone can mangle a sentence badly but you can still come away with the meaning of their speech most of the time. Kind of like how this book is written as a rambling stream of consciousness, but you're still vibing with it. Right?

Right?

Relating this idea to heuristics more specifically, gestaltism shows us that we see things as an overall image before breaking them down into their constituent parts.

Psi here is portrayed as a stereotypical tough-as-nails miscreant. That's the immediate impression we get, and upon further analysis we can point to details such as the skull necklace, the sunglasses, the angry expression, and the body language that contribute to the overall image of a tough cookie. Now look at this:

Bam. With this different depiction of the same Psi, we are now forced to re-evaluate their identity. We can now describe them as a "ruffian with a soft spot for nature." But look at the phraseology used here—we're still stereotyping Psi but adding a stipulation. We still see Psi as a package deal of traits (as much as the knowledge of their animal friends has swayed our view of them) using the stereotype of a "tough person" as a baseline template. It is upon that template we fill in details that may either contribute to or detract from the pure essence of the stereotype, but, in the end, if Psi shows us that they are 70 percent something, we mostly assume the unseen 30 percent won't need to be accounted for, as it's unlikely to change Psi's overall image so drastically that it becomes something else entirely.

Storytellers use this all the time in media. There's a reason character tropes exist. You'll usually see similar characters across different movies or books or shows—"the nerd," "the boring schoolteacher," "the caring parent," "the goofball"—this isn't because the people making these characters are unoriginal; usage of stereotypical characters (with some unique traits to make them memorable) provides the audience with some immediate context of what to expect from them so we aren't left completely in the dark. The intricacies of their motivations, backstory, and quirks can be left for the audience to figure out later, but having some sort of framework within which to see their actions helps us not be frantically and constantly trying and failing to evaluate every situation they're in to get a read on them.

At this point I wouldn't blame you if you were thinking something like, "Well, make up your mind already! Are you trying to say heuristics are good or bad?" There are arguments in both directions to be sure, and while it'd be disingenuously faux-intellectual of me to be an "enlightened centrist" in this situation, it can't be avoided that there's a legitimate mix of benefit and concern here.

STEREOTYPES INCREASING PROCESSING SPEED

It's true that letting our minds file things into categories is useful for quick, on-the-fly organizing, and you bet it would have helped our tree-dwelling ancestors in life-or-death snap-judgment situations. In a civilized society like ours, however, it's apparent why certain things like stereotyping can present problems. Coming up is some research that identifies how baked-in some of our biases are, even if we try our best not to let them cloud our judgment. Culturally, we've made great strides in deprogramming general prejudices regarding things like ethnicity, religion, sexual identity, and economic background (to name a few); this is thanks to the efforts of many conscious individuals. However, some ideas perpetuated by societal stereotypes persist in the overarching consciousness of society. It's important to note that the following research is not a statement of endorsement for any ideology and simply an explanation of phenomena that present themselves in the real world.

Jennifer Eberhardt, psychology professor at Stanford University, wanted to see the power of implicit bias structures when it came to looking at people of various races—in particular, her work that we'll be touching on was focused on African American faces versus European-American faces. One of the earlier findings was that members of both races were more likely to recognize and distinguish people in their race and had a markedly more difficult time identifying people of the other race.

More socially relevant were her experiments on how this could affect criminal justice. She figured if these implicit biases were so strong that they impacted perception, wouldn't it be reasonably inferred that some important legal judgment calls were also impacted by this?

To test this, Eberhardt had a bunch of college students try to identify a blurry image, like this.

Then, slowly, she had the image increase in resolution and the participants were asked to blurt out what the object was as soon as they could recognize it.

Oh dear—it's a gun.

Now there's a plot twist to all this (you'll find that psychology experiments often have some sort of plot twist). Before the image identification activity began, Eberhardt blipped an image on-screen to the experiment participants. The image being blipped was one of three things: a picture of a white person, a picture of a Black person, or some random amorphous shape. And when I say "blip," I mean the image lasted for such a short time that no human mind could consciously process what it had just seen.

Shockingly, Eberhardt found the participants were faster at identifying the object as a gun if they were exposed to the picture of the Black person right before the test. This doesn't mean they're racist or carry biased beliefs—their subconscious took over and tried to make associations to complete the task, whether they were associations that these people would ever consciously make or agree with. It's possible that even so much as having heard of stereotypes associating certain ethnicities to certain crimes could have been enough for their brains to make the association—it might be a grasp for straws on the brain's part, but it shows it became part of the programming.

When I say heuristics are useful, am I advocating for stereotyping people based on their demographic data? Of course not. We have to examine if the heuristics we use are justified, and that begins by recognizing they are present in the first place. This is as important as it is difficult, however—it's asking you to evaluate something you didn't know you didn't know. A lot of the time, you don't know what you don't know, you know? And even if we do know the heuristic is there, can we hope to deprogram ourselves by willing it to be so? It'd be hard and humbling, but we can get there with practice and awareness.

EXPERIENCE MAY BETRAY

"How reliable is your background knowledge?"

This isn't a trick question, so just answer what you think instinctually in good faith: do you think people are generally more scared of dogs than sharks? Probably not, right? If you surveyed a thousand random people and asked them to categorize sharks and dogs into "scary" and "not scary," you'd get a hefty majority of people categorizing sharks into "scary" and dogs into "not scary."

This may not surprise you if you think about it for more than a few seconds, but there are far more dog attacks and fatalities on humans per year than those by sharks. Like, we're talking a single-digit number of shark attack-induced deaths versus tens of thousands of dog-induced deaths per year on average. It's common knowledge by now that sharks don't like messing with people and find us kind of unappetizing. So why are we way more scared of swimming and potentially getting bitten by a shark versus walking outside on the street and potentially getting bitten by a dog even though the latter happens exceedingly more often?

THE AVAILABILITY HEURISTIC

Step right up, step right up, folks; allow me to introduce to you the handy-dandy availability heuristic!

Indeed, with this newfangled gadget of unprecedented mental facilitation, you too can spare yourself the labors of thought. Want to assess the probability of succeeding as a technology company CEO after dropping out of university? Look no further than famous examples of people who did just that, like Bill Gates and Mark Zuckerberg—since they did it, that should mean it's likely...right?

The obvious answer is that no, of course it's extraordinarily unlikely for someone to become an uber-successful tech CEO right out of college, let alone right after dropping out. But because we can immediately think of examples like these, it suddenly doesn't seem so out-of-reach anymore. Same with shark attacks—we are more likely to fear a shark attack happening to us on vacation instead of a dog attack while taking a walk, because it's easier to immediately bring to mind the imagery of a shark attack and you've presumably seen more mean depictions of sharks than of dogs (whether or not they're being accurately proportionally represented).

The availability heuristic is our tendency to assess probabilities based on how easily examples come to mind. This doesn't necessarily mean we make stoic judgments about how likely things are based on how many examples we have. It means we act in a way that might be disproportionately cognizant of the implications of a certain result occurring from an event, based on how fast our brain makes the association between the event and the potential result. This could be due to how bombastic or dramatic the result is or how often one thinks about the event. People are more likely to be afraid of flying on planes than being a passenger in a car, even if traffic accidents occur at a way higher rate than aviation accidents. This is because it's easier to quickly associate planes with crashing. We usually aren't thinking about planes except when we hear that one crashed or see one in a movie (usually being blown up), so that association can become faster in people's minds. Meanwhile, a lot of people think about cars every day, but it's in the context of more mundane stuff like, "Gotta fill up the gas," or, "I'll save thirty minutes of walking if I take the car," or, "That guy just cut me off (seriously rude)!"

THE REPRESENTATIVENESS HEURISTIC

That's not all when it comes to heuristics messing up our ability to calculate or make guesses. Look at this Psi here. What occupation do you think Psi has?

If you guessed "pilot," I'm sorry, but you're incorrect. Psi is a truck driver. Why did you make that guess?

You probably guessed something like a pilot because you looked at the clues Psi gave us with the clothes and surroundings. Your brain did a quick cross-reference of which stereotypical representative it most closely resembles and went, "We have a 90 percent match between this Psi and what I imagine as the stereotypical representation of a pilot—Psi is probably a pilot." That's right; your brain used Psi's compatibility with a "representation" to assess what it was looking at—this is called the representativeness heuristic.

Like the availability heuristic, the representativeness heuristic is an assessment of probabilities. The computer in your mind goes, "Okay, I need to make a correct guess here; how can I increase my chances of getting it right based on the description or details given to me?" and proceeds to evaluate how well the guess lines up with stereotypes already present or that can be conjured up—the important thing is that you will often be comparing to things you're easily able to cite representatives of and not accounting for the raw probability of the alternatives. You can maybe see how that could lead to inaccurate calculations from a pure statistics standpoint.

That explanation may have flown right over your head ("flown," like a pilot, haha), so allow me to cite an example from a famous experiment by Daniel Kahneman and Amos Tversky. The two psychologists set out on their research to see how people make predictions (and "making predictions" is another way of saying "assessing the most likely outcome"—i.e., looking at probabilities). They asked students to judge a made-up student named Tom W., who was described as follows:

- Highly intelligent, but lacking creativity

- Orderly and neat with an emphasis on performing duties well

- Introverted and unemotional

- Is a sci-fi kinda guy

The psychologists asked one group of students to judge how much Tom fit into the "stereotype" of a student of the various faculties.

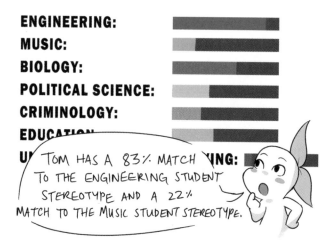

ENGINEERING:
MUSIC:
BIOLOGY:
POLITICAL SCIENCE:
CRIMINOLOGY:
EDUCATION
U **ING:**

TOM HAS A 83% MATCH TO THE ENGINEERING STUDENT STEREOTYPE AND A 22% MATCH TO THE MUSIC STUDENT STEREOTYPE.

They then asked another group of students to judge how likely Tom was to be a student of each faculty.

ENGINEERING:
MUSIC:
BIOLOGY:
POLITICAL SCIENCE:
CRIMINOLOGY:
EDUCATION:
UNDERW **AVING:**

MY BEST GUESS IS THAT TOM IS ENROLLED HERE...

Finally, they asked a last group of students how likely any given student would be in any faculty based on enrollment data. This one isn't an opinion, really. It's kind of just math.

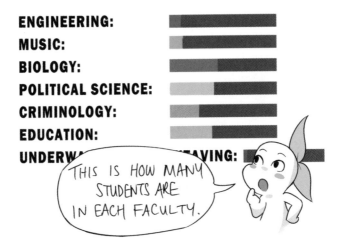

ENGINEERING:
MUSIC:
BIOLOGY:
POLITICAL SCIENCE:
CRIMINOLOGY:
EDUCATION:
UNDERW... ...VING:

THIS IS HOW MANY STUDENTS ARE IN EACH FACULTY.

Well, survey says despite the comparatively low chance that any student would happen to be in engineering if you randomly selected an individual in the school, most of the students predicted Tom would be in engineering. The "stereotype matching" group shows us that it's entirely due to how much Tom reminded them of "typical" engineering students, rare as they are.

With these findings, Kahneman and Tversky developed the idea that people are drawn to conclusions that feed off their experiences and intuition in lieu of statistical evidence. We're more likely to predict rare outcomes due to representativeness. When I asked you what job Psi has, you were *way* more likely to be correct by randomly guessing "truck driver" than "pilot," due to the sheer number of truck drivers being vastly higher than the number of pilots. At least in the United States anyway. Maybe if you're in a country with a plane infestation and where trucks are extinct, the story might be different. In that case, okay, you win; Psi is a pilot. Statistically speaking, of course.

It's easy to get the availability heuristic and representative heuristic confused, so let me provide a neat little visual to distinguish the two, because they're different:

They are different concepts entirely, but they both show us how our minds can take easy shortcuts to establish a story about the world and our past even if it's not true or likely. The goal isn't accuracy but creating a view of the world and a way of living that makes enough sense.

READING BETWEEN THE LINES

"Are you paying attention to a house or the bricks?"

Imagine this scene in a movie: storm clouds roll in, it starts raining, it's super dark, the dramatic music plays. The scene shifts over to the main character sitting alone in a cafe. Put yourself in this character's shoes—how do you feel right now?

Happy, right? No? Sorry, I don't know why I guessed that. Maybe it's because I'm not under the influence of the Kuleshov Effect!

THE KULESHOV EFFECT

What is the Kuleshov Effect? I'm glad you asked. In return, I will answer. The Kuleshov Effect is honestly more of a cinematography concept than a psychology concept, but it's being brought up because it shows how powerful implicit perception is to our understanding of the phenomenological world. It is a technique that uses a sequence of images to force viewers to make a connection and therefore attributes emotions or meaning to figures that otherwise would not carry these associations if shown on their own. This illustrates our tendency to work backward from context clues rather than the direct explicit visuals being presented. This means that this scene:

...can mean different things when you put it in sequence with different images. Observe:

The isolated scene itself is the same. All that was changed were the surrounding context clues!

Of course, the idea that people's interpretations of events can be influenced by the order in which they are presented is not anything novel. You know how in school, they tell you to write essays by putting your strongest points in the beginning and end, leaving the weakest points in the middle? That certainly isn't unfounded advice. Unbeknownst to you, you learned to apply the Primacy Effect and the Recency Effect. Or maybe it was beknownst to you because you are a genius whiz kid who already knew the names of these phenomena. I'm almost certain "beknownst" is not an actual word.

THE PRIMACY EFFECT & RECENCY EFFECT

The Primacy Effect describes how we tend to strongly remember things by their first impression—whether it's the opening to a speech, the first paragraph of an essay, or the first minutes of a movie. One way we apply the Primacy Effect in the internet business at Psych2Go is making sure the first few seconds of all of our videos are dynamic, eye-catching, and have a snappy, attention-catching or thought-provoking line in the narration right away. This works to admittedly...varying degrees...but that's more of an execution thing than a theory thing. Looking at our video analytics hammers in the importance of a strong start to a video.

Having the first thirty seconds of a video be a ten out of ten in quality leaves people with the impression that the entire video was a ten out of ten, even though perhaps the quality after the intro drops off to a seven or eight out of ten. That's your daily internet clout tip. Remember me when you become a famous influencer!

The recency effect, similarly, is our tendency to give more bias or attribute more importance to recent events than is justified by history. This kind of applies to the essay thing again; just like how primacy effects make the beginning of an essay memorable, the most recent thing you read (i.e., the ending) will also hold a lot more weight than, say, the middle. I'd venture to guess that you've heard the phrases "start off strong" or "end with a bang" before—these phrases are cliches because they're effective!

To bring some science to the recency effect, Wändi Bruine de Bruin, professor at the University of Southern California, examined how a judge panel might evaluate things differently based on presentation order. She found that figure skating competitors, whose performances are evaluated one by one, tended to receive higher scores if they performed later. And if you're reading this while also being familiar with international figure skating competition protocol, you may be a little confused as to why this is surprising—after all, performance order is based on how good you are; the better you score, the later you perform. However, this is only true for the second round—international figure skating consists of two rounds, with the first round's performance order completely random. In both rounds, the finding remained consistent—the advantage of going later was tangible.

Maybe this is why in movies involving a big performance competition, like a dance battle or a singing contest, the main character usually always goes last and wins the whole thing. Not only is the main character subtly manipulating the judges' perceptions to appear better than they are, but it also reinforces to us, the audience, that this is supposed to be "the good performance." Didn't we discuss another movie trick where they use context and clever sequencing of scenes to imply emotion and meaning? That's right; this isn't entirely detached from the Kuleshov Effect. It's all connected, y'know? Our perceptions are constantly influenced by the randomest things and it all cooks together to give us a picture of the world that's gone through a few creative liberties.

LASER FOCUS

**"If a tree falls in a forest and no one is there to hear it,
should it have done it louder?"**

Okay, okay, what if I don't want my attention swayed by such trifles as the order of presentation or involuntary consumption of ancillary stimuli? Can't I block out the noise and zero in on what I want? Surely, subordinate to our instincts as we are, we humans can manage *some* sort of agency regarding concentration?

If that's your concern, I have some good news and I have some bad news. Which one do you want to hear first?

What if I said both at the same time? Which one would you try to catch?

Here, I'll write the good news in red and the bad news in blue.

Did you get that? How!? Isn't that a mess of scribbles overlapping with each other? How did you make out a legible sentence from that? You were somehow able to separate them in your mind... But how?

THE COCKTAIL PARTY EFFECT

What you just experienced was an attempt to visually represent what's known as the Cocktail Party Effect. Scientist Collin Cherry was the one who came up with the term as he investigated people's ability to selectively attend to one conversation among many, even in a noisy environment—say, a cocktail party. Yeah, come to think of it, how can we hear our conversation partner in loud environments with louder noises around us, including other people's words that could get mixed in with the ones we're trying to hear?

Turns out, our brains are decent at *not* paying attention on command—just enough to at least focus on something else, anyway.

Cherry found a lot of fun things about how selective attention works—he found that participants in an experiment could successfully listen exclusively to one message being played on one ear of a pair of headphones even if it was overlaid with a different message in the other ear. The only time people were kind of "snapped out of it" was when the "irrelevant" message suddenly mentioned the participant's name—this diverted their attention at least enough to detect their name had been spoken.

"GOOD" "DOG" "TOY" "TIME"

"PAT" "THE" "PSI" "HEAD"

We see this sort of selective attention often used in the real world—aside from the cocktail party example, there's also a use case for this capability in babies. The fact that babies can focus on the sound of their parents' voices through other noises and even other voices suggests that this ability is learned at an early age or may even be innate. It should be noted, however, that you get better and better at filtering stuff as you age (and then you get a little worse at it when you get real old).

So how good are we at homing in on one message or stimulus? Pretty decent, honestly, unless some stimulus in the "ignored" portion of your input suddenly gets labeled as "important"—whether it's because your name was mentioned or the stimulus was loud, strange, or directly interfered with the "important" input, or what have you. But how direct does the interference have to be to start interfering? If I'm trying to do my listening test and you start repeatedly punching me in the face, will I remember the words as "BAM, BAM, BAM, BAM" instead? Not quite. Uhhh, that is, let's not find out.

The line for what counts as "interference" is a little more abstract than that. Psychologists Jeffrey Alan Gray and Alexander A.I. Wedderburn conducted an experiment like Cherry did with the headphones. This time, however, they had a set of one-syllable words playing in one ear while another set of one-syllable words played in the other and asked participants to list the words being spoken from one ear only. They found that, if mixing the words from different ears together would create a coherent sentence or phrase, participants would sometimes recall this phrase as being what they heard.Consistent with what we know about gestaltism, this reveals that we tend to perceive "meaning" holistically, rather than perceiving constituents before deriving meaning from their assemblage after the fact.

THE ELDERLY ELEVATOR EXPERIMENT

Here's some stuff that might put all this "unintentional perception" stuff into perspective. Psychologists John A. Bargh, Mark Chen, and Lara Burrows wanted to see how powerful the effects of priming were. Priming is when something prepares you to think about things a certain way by incidentally activating the thought structures surrounding it. For example, if you're shown pictures of cows and then are subsequently asked to name a drink, you'll probably say "milk." Previous thoughts and perceptions have a passive, lingering effect on how you perceive things afterward— even if what happens afterward is completely unrelated. Remember the blurry gun experiment? That was a **prime** example of priming. (Badum tss!)

Bargh, Chen, and Burrows wanted to find evidence that, not only was automatic priming from stimuli that you didn't know you were affected by a real thing, but it could also impact more than your active thought processes. They were interested in investigating the **principle of ideomotor action** (you don't have to remember that), which means thinking about an action makes you more likely to do it. They figured since the precursor to behavior was thought, and if perception can prime us for thought, then maybe sometimes the thought that precludes behavior doesn't need to come from us. What if instead of the thought coming from our minds, we outsourced it to come from a perception?

Bargh, Chen, and Burrows conducted an experiment where they had participants unscramble randomly assorted words to form proper sentences. They didn't tell them the participants were split into three groups—one group received words having to do with "rudeness" (such as "bother," "disturb," "annoyingly"), another received "polite" words (like "courteous" and "patiently"), and a third control group received random, neutral words (like "normally").

They told the participants to find the experimenter in another room after finishing the task. When the participants went to find them, however, the experimenter would be busy having a conversation with someone that looked like another participant. Secretly, the experimenter was timing how long it would take for participants to interrupt the conversation and—surprise, surprise—the "rude" group would interrupt significantly faster than either of the other groups.

Our trio of psychologists then explored the idea further with another similar experiment. The same word scramble task was given to participants, but this time, one group was given words related to the concept of "elderly." After participants had finished the task, experimenters secretly timed how long the participants took to walk to the elevator to exit the area. Lo and behold, the group that had received "elderly" words walked slower than the group that had received neutral words. It's not like the slower group had received words related to slowness either—the mere association of "elderly" and the tendency to move slightly slower was enough to affect participants' behavior.

As much as we think our actions are dictated by discrete chunks of logic (e.g., "I am hungry; therefore it would be wise to go to the burger joint to get food"), these chunks of logic are not free of being sprinkled with the essence of our surroundings (maybe you think you're hungry because you are standing in your dining room?) and the course of action decided is also influenced (maybe you could eat something healthy that you have in your fridge, but seeing all those cow pictures earlier suddenly got you thinking of burgers).

YOU REAP WHAT YOU SOW

"Can what we do retroactively impact what we think?"

We've talked extensively about how input can affect processing and how processing can affect output. But what if I told you that even output can influence processing? I know arrows were going unidirectionally in the computer diagram thing at the beginning of the section, but again—we're not dealing with a computer here; we're dealing with an entire brain. It's always a little difficult and maybe a little frustrating to hear explanations in supposedly solid terms only to be told that there are levels of uninformed nuance clouding things, but believe me, you should see how much grief that causes the researchers themselves. When you don't have clear answers like in arithmetic and everything in your field of study is on a sliding scale of "usually" and "most of the time"... Well, I'm not saying this statistic is related, but there could be a reason as to why it's been found that up to 85 percent of therapists have therapists.

How exactly is output influencing our minds? Am I going to go into talking about reinforced neural pathways and the like? No. At least, not directly. Not for now. Dun dun dun. As much as many of us would like to believe that the world happens *at* us while we sit there and take it, we dish as much into the void as we take from it. Our output is part of that "world" we're taking in.

THE WHORFIAN HYPOTHESIS

If you're bilingual, this may be something you've noticed, but the way language is poised is an important factor in how you express yourself, think of certain things, and, yes, perceive the world around you. As an example, in Korean, the word for *eel* approximates, in its etymology, "long fish." This is as opposed to in English where eels are called, well, eels. Though a lot of people may know eels are a fish, usually in the English-speaking West, we typically categorize eels more distally from traditional, fish-shaped fish. Already you can see how this might inform biases of things like how likely one would be willing to try to eat an eel. A "long fish" sounds appetizing—like, yeah, we eat fish all the time! Eating a long one means more fish! But eating an "eel"? Eh...I dunno... I think I gotta go...catch a bus... or something...

It's not that people speaking Korean are intentionally trying to make eels more appetizing or artificially expand the common definition of "fish," but perhaps the etymology of the word most used to describe the phenomenon has been implicitly affecting the pattern of thought used to perceive it.

Whatever the reason, it can be seen how this kind of thing could have even the slightest effect. Whether the specific example I used truly has the exact impact that I described is not important; it's being cited to illustrate a point.

Looking at the etymology of words in different languages can reveal the beautiful differences in how their namers viewed them!

Enter the Whorfian Hypothesis, named after Benjamin Lee Whorf, an American linguist, anthropologist, and Taurus (if you care, I guess), interested in looking at the effect language had on thought and how we structured our understanding of reality. The idea is also referred to as linguistic relativity, but "Whorfian Hypothesis" is more clickbait-y and sounds like it could be the title of an episode of *Star Trek*.

The hypothesis, as far as its tenets go, is something like this: the structure of language informs thought, perception, and the development of conceptual knowledge. It can be derived from this, then, that those who speak different languages may have different cognitive processes altogether.

The legitimacy of the hypothesis is contested because many of the examples used to support it either lack scientific thoroughness in analyzing other confounding factors or are logically tenuous. Controversial an idea as it remains to this day, it does offer an interesting insight into how it could be possible that the means of output we are constrained to dictate how the "processing" and "storage" stages of how the brain-computer works. For example, if someone asks you to describe what the color "red" looks like, you'd be hard-pressed to do so, not because you don't know what red is, but because you are limited in your expression. You settle with some roundabout answer that doesn't address the appearance of red in any objective way. If someone steps on your foot, your output is limited such that you can't breathe fire in response, no matter how hard you try or how angry you are. You settle with something like screaming as loud as possible and internally wishing ill fortune upon the foot-stepper.

A more practical, albeit speculative, takeaway from this is that we are limited in output to what we have at our disposal—so it'd be good practice for us all to be cautious about the words we use. Using harsh words all the time might cause us to think in extremes more often, and using vague speech might make us less confident.

Another common example is ranting—it's been shown that being a complainer often will lead individuals to reinforce their negative feelings and the action rarely helps in the long term. It's important to expand your toolkit as much as possible to become well-rounded! Learn how to compliment people in your voice so it doesn't sound unnatural! Speak nice words for beautiful lips! Eat your vegetables! Blah blah blah.

THE MISINFORMATION EFFECT

We've seen now that merely how we talk about things can impact how we think about them. How far can this reprogramming go, though? A somewhat more sinister (or funny, depending on how you look at it) application of the capability to disrupt one's perception processing by changing the output is found in the misinformation effect.

While it's easy to make cute little mistakes due to heuristics clouding our judgment, sometimes the consequences of doing so can be drastic and long-term. The misinformation effect is a phenomenon that sort of feeds off of our tendency to use these heuristics and makes people believe in false or misleading things. Not because arguments for these false or misleading bits of information are strong or appeal to these heuristics—it's simpler than that. We can be influenced to remember incorrect information by merely being exposed to it. This is especially true if we're frequently exposed to the same lie.

The misinformation effect can not only add fake memories that get integrated with our actual experiences, but it can overwrite our existing memories with different ones. The idea that our ability to recall events is impeded by things that happen after the event (e.g., someone feeding you made-up details about it) is a tangential display of heuristics at work. You don't remember things by bringing forth a perfect image of the past as it happened—you "remember" things by hastily reconstructing that image in your mind. After reconstruction, you take a look at the hodgepodge recreation that your mind made and settle for that. Problem is, to make that reconstruction, your brain will just use whatever's at its disposal—including whatever garbage information it can find adjacent to the memory that might not even be accurate. Whether that scene you're retelling consists of a pure account of things or if there are flecks of random, inaccurate tidbits you didn't actually see (but were influenced into thinking you saw), you can't be too sure.

A famous experiment looking at the misinformation effect was conducted by psychologists Elizabeth Loftus and John C. Palmer to examine how much one could exactly get away with when it came to feeding imaginary details. The experimenters showed participants of the experiment a clip of a vehicle collision. Afterward, they were asked how fast the cars were going. However, it's important to note that this was asked in one of five different ways:

- How fast were the cars going when they *hit* each other?

- How fast were the cars going when they *smashed* into each other?

- How fast were the cars going when they *collided* with each other?

- How fast were the cars going when they *bumped* into each other?

- How fast were the cars going when they *contacted* each other?

There was a demonstrable change in perception in the participants depending on what particular phrasing was used: people asked about the cars "contacting" each other gave the slowest estimates while people asked about the cars "smashing" each other gave the highest estimates. By asking the participants about cars "smashing into each other," the seed of a narrative is already established—the accident is assumed to be a "smash." Amusingly, the speed of the cars witnessed didn't change the results.

A week later, the effects of the misinformation effect persisted—in fact, maybe they crystallized the memories to be harder-coded after being modified when they were most malleable. When participants were asked whether they saw shattered glass in the footage, the "smashed into each other" group was more likely to answer that they did see it—even though there was no shattered glass! The reasoning for this was interpreted to be that since a "smashing" accident would be more likely to yield broken glass, the participants filled in their memory gaps with the nonexistent detail since it made sense with the narrative in their head.

Making good and correct calls is more difficult than you'd think. Forget about entire accounts of car crashes for a moment—even the smaller, calculative efforts we do such as making predictions or external judgments often rely on mental shortcuts, leading to major errors. The lesson here is to be mindful of our perceptions and seek additional information before making decisions. Knowing and accepting that we may come up short from time to time because it's impossible to account for everything, we understand that that too is part of the learning process. Take the punch like a champ and roll with it! Just make sure you perceive the punch so you can properly acknowledge it.

CHAPTER 2

WORKING HARD OR HARDLY WORKING?

MOTIVATION AND PRODUCTIVITY

While this book isn't supposed to be strictly "self-help," if it can assist you, lovely reader, that would be awesome. We will be talking about how productivity works, so if you're not a conscientious individual, some of this section might read like it's calling you out. Trust me; the last thing we want to do is make you feel like you're being nagged (by a *book*, of all things). We're not in the business of giving unsolicited life advice that you already know deep down; you know, the obvious stuff like, "Do work instead of watching TV for higher productivity." What we *can* do, though, is give you unsolicited life advice *with scientific context*! I bet you'd listen to other people's nagging more if they cited their sources.

We have a sort of obligation to ourselves regarding productivity, which you've probably felt any time you got mad at yourself for procrastinating on a school assignment. Where does the reaction of getting angry at oneself come from, genetically speaking? Why are we programmed to feel this sense of shame or guilt when we haven't met the expectations of productivity set out for us?

Industriousness is a trait marked by being good at listening to instructions, buckling down and carrying out tasks on time, and being consistent. Those sound like unconditionally great traits to have—after all, those traits are what school tries to train you in. Indeed, industriousness is a massive predictor of long-term life success and it's not hard to imagine why. If that's the case, though, why have we not evolved as a species to be biologically completely 100 percent amazingly diligent at all times? If it's such an important quality, it should've been stamped into our DNA, right? Because I mean, clearly, we can evolve out of certain behaviors if they aren't desired in society. For example, some animals eat their own poop, but we'd never do that—and not strictly because of social taboos but because nobody *wants* to. I'm not accepting any arguments on that.

It turns out that being hyper-work-focused comes with a smorgasbord of pitfalls. It's hard to relax, you might be too hard on yourself, you're more inflexible, you get stressed at things more lax individuals wouldn't mind, and sometimes, maybe most importantly, working hard doesn't necessarily net you the most benefit.

Have you heard the phrase "work smarter, not harder"? It means that figuring out how to work efficiently and more directly toward a goal is often more effective than mindlessly hacking away at a problem, sacrificing time, strength, or both. A lot of self-proclaimed "lazy" successful people attribute their success in a diligent person's world to the fact that their laziness forces them to find ways to get things done quickly so they don't have to work as hard.

One theory as to why non-industrious genes remain in our DNA is related to our ability to plan for the future. For industrious people who value stability, they are investing in a future that they hope looks like the present. Slow but consistent incremental contributions paint a nice, smooth picture of the future where hard work paid off proportionately to what was invested. You can think of this as someone who makes small payments into a fund every month. However, if that fund happens to collapse or society gets rocked by some great catastrophe, suddenly the structure they so dearly held on to is dissolved and the people who can milk the chaotic circumstances are the winners—the less industrious, more adaptable crowd.

Society needs a balance of all types of players in all different areas to have well-rounded diversity of ideas. Widening your range on the spectrum of industriousness is always good—it makes you capable of expressing diligent and laid-back attitudes whenever the situation calls for one or the other.

The prevailing problem for most people, even some industrious individuals, is the inability to get to work and make that work count. You can probably think of a few people you consider as "responsible," and I'd bet they still sometimes have problems with time management or productivity. It could be said, though, that for a lot of people it's not a lack of ability to be responsible but a lack of knowledge on how to access the ability. For some it can come naturally, sure, but in the case of those for whom it doesn't, the luck of the draw is such that it'll have to be a conscious process for the time being. That is, until it becomes a habit (which it can)!

Whether you read this next section as advice, insight into how the brain handles the concepts of motivation and productivity, or fun trivia facts, that's up to you. Regardless, it's about high time we see what we can do about this industriousness spectrum!

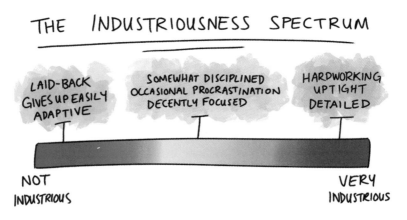

THE INDUSTRIOUSNESS SPECTRUM

LAID-BACK GIVES UP EASILY ADAPTIVE

SOMEWHAT DISCIPLINED OCCASIONAL PROCRASTINATION DECENTLY FOCUSED

HARDWORKING UPTIGHT DETAILED

NOT INDUSTRIOUS

VERY INDUSTRIOUS

BE POLITE,
BE EFFICIENT,
AND HAVE A PLAN

"Can't we put off talking about procrastination
until a bit later?"

Nobody is kidding themselves when they procrastinate. We know it's bad and will come back to bite us; it happens time and time again and we never learn. This seems like a massive flaw in reasoning and even goes against what we know about human behavior—you'd think a habit with that much negative reinforcement would be phased out in an instant after getting burned by it a few times—but you and I both know that procrastination can be a lifelong concern.

Procrastination can feel like an ever-looming, almost transcendent force and its tendrils can reach so deep that they are undetectable. You know what they say—the invisible demons are the deadliest. Nobody says that. I made that up. But it's true that it's hard to plan to tackle something if you can't even size it up—if only someone made a formula for calculating motivation so we could combat procrastination more clinically!

...what do you mean they did exactly that?

TEMPORAL MOTIVATION THEORY

$$\text{MOTIVATION} = \frac{\text{EXPECTANCY} \times \text{VALUE}}{1 + (\text{IMPULSIVENESS} \times \text{DELAY})}$$

I want to say this formula looks almost satirical at first glance, but this is real. This looks like something I would write as an overly convoluted joke to a friend who asks me what I think the formula to success is. This is in no way a knock against its validity, however—this is an idea developed by Piers Steel and Cornelius J. König, professors investigating the science of procrastination, as part of temporal motivation theory (or TMT for short). Breaking the formula down, you can see how it makes a lot of sense and helps us better grasp what we're dealing with regarding how much our motivation fights with our procrastination.

We won't spend too long on this since I doubt you opened this book to do math, but we'll briefly go through the variables one by one:

- **Expectancy:** The likelihood of success. You can substitute this with "confidence" if you want. Motivation is higher if this is higher.

- **Value:** How much you care about what you're doing. This is tied to how big the reward for completion is. Motivation is higher if this is higher.

- **Impulsiveness:** How bad you are at delaying gratification—the opposite of discipline. Motivation is lower if this is higher.

- **Delay:** How long it'll take to see the benefit of doing the thing/ how much time you have left to do it (most of the time these are the same thing). You can also think of this as "how far away is the due date" when talking about school assignments. Motivation is lower if this is higher.

The interesting part about this is that time is a factor in motivation. Hence the "temporal" part of "temporal motivation theory." That's the least intuitive part of all this, but it offers a fascinating insight into what suddenly pushes us to do the entire essay in one night as if we got hit with a lightning bolt of inspiration. It seems that how sensitive we are to the "delay" part of the equation has a big impact on the severity of the procrastination.

TMT doesn't just deal with motivation—it also acts as a sorting method that tells us how we prioritize tasks. It stands to reason that we prioritize what we're more motivated to do, as they're almost functionally the same thing in this instance. If for example you have two things to do, and they have equal expectancy and value, then the only thing that separates the two is delay (since impulsiveness doesn't vary from task to task). You can see this in action if you have two tasks due but one of them is further away—you want to do the one that's coming up sooner first.

You can see then that knowledge of our priorities being shaped by our internal temporal motivation circuits helps us understand the specific factors about a task preventing us from acting. It allows us to objectivize the situation and go, "Am I delaying progress in this task because I don't believe in my ability to do it? Is it because I don't believe in the value? Is it because I need to be more disciplined?" Understanding the principles of TMT can help us to develop strategies to overcome procrastination. And if you've never *not* procrastinated before, let me tell you as a former chronic procrastinator, it feels *really* good.

IN THE ZONE (A.K.A. FLOW STATE)

If you've ever had to cut wrapping paper, you'll know that sometimes your scissors suddenly hit that perfect spot where you can suddenly start just gliding it in maximum overdrive to cut the rest of the way through with minimal effort. This is a pretty decent way of visualizing what psychologist Mihály Csíkszentmihályi (pronounced "mee-high cheek-sent-mee-high"), looked into regarding the concept of "flow." You know, like when you're working on something and it just feels like you're "in the zone." Like if you've ever been practicing on an instrument and you have a really long streak of playing without any mistakes, it kind of feels very similar to the scissor glide-y zone thing.

"Flow" is the term used in positive psychology (the branch of psychology that looks at ways to make life happier) to describe when you're immersed in what you're doing—it's like you're in a trance. You can tell you're in a flow state if it seems like your perception of time is distorted—time will have passed faster than how it felt. Flow state allows for extended periods of effortless concentration, but it's critical that the activity being performed is somewhat enjoyable or satisfying. It might be a little hard to describe if you've never experienced it, but it's quite a common experience for many people and is a great way to relieve stress or boredom.

It should be noted that this is separate from hyperfocus, when one becomes absorbed in a task to the point of neglecting other needs and is often detrimental to one's well-being. Flow, in contrast, is usually seen as a good thing. Hyperfocus can make you feel guilty or tired afterward, while flow should usually feel fulfilling, like a serendipitous encounter with a particularly satisfying sheet of wrapping paper.

There are a few prerequisites to achieve flow state—it doesn't randomly activate sometimes while doing tasks for a long time. There isn't a universally agreed-upon, strict list of what needs to be done or present to reach flow, but here are a few commonly cited requirements:

- The individual must have a goal.

- The task must be productive.

- The task should be at a difficulty level appropriately relative to the individual's skill.

- The individual should be in an environment of reduced distractions.

All of these points are of practical relevance to someone who may be seeking to achieve a flow state. Listing these factors makes it easier to see what parameters can be adjusted for someone unable to tap into a flow state. For example, if someone is too bored with the task to achieve flow, the difficulty may be too low—adjusting this, Csíkszentmihályi says, may help refine the task to be more conducive to achieving flow. So now that you know the basics behind it, next time you get into a flow state, make a note of it and hold whatever you were doing near and dear to you!

THE SCIENCE OF STRESS

"Why bother with being bothered?"

In the media world, where Psych2Go happens to be active, we know to get audiences engaged in our content, there has to be some sort of hook. When our viewers feel invested all the way through one of our videos or articles, it's usually because we've intrinsically introduced some sort of narrative to them with a certain level of stakes. Stakes make or break! If you flip a coin, don't you want to see what side it landed on? Or better yet—don't you want to see if you guessed it right?

When you feel like something's on the line, the entire game changes. You will play a competitive game differently if there's a prize for winning, and you're **definitely** going to play differently if there's a penalty for losing. Pressure is a huge factor in motivation, which we sort of tangentially covered in the previous section with the TMT formula. There's a small difference in nuance here, though—TMT tells us that we prioritize things coming up sooner or have better rewards, all other things being equal, while what we're talking about right now is how the experience of feeling pressure or stress is a factor in motivation.

But what if it's more than just motivation being affected? What if that feeling of being pushed to our limits actually, well, pushes us to our limits? Stress, despite seeming like a more abstract concept, is well-understood biologically. The various bodily components of stress, like hormones and neurotransmitters, and the sort of electric and kinetic activity associated with the stress response are all things that researchers have a surprisingly decent grasp on.

FIGHT OR FLIGHT

Why does stress exist in the first place? Why are humans built to not only be capable of stress, but easily susceptible to it? Well, like we talked about with the industriousness spectrum before, sometimes you need a little bit of this and a little bit of that.

We need to back up when talking about stress because it's only half of the story. There's that heart-thumping, doom-calling, sweat-inducing stress, but you may have also heard of "good stress." People are referring to the concept of "arousal" when they say this. You may have heard that term used in conversation regarding sexual attraction, but we're using the word in the scientific meaning. Arousal is a state of heightened alertness to prepare for action—this can kind of sound like regular-old stress, but it can be a response to something exciting or fun, like sports or challenges.

Stress is like the evil twin brother of arousal. Similar things are happening, like the release of hormones such as adrenaline, but for all the worst reasons. Maybe you are in a dangerous situation (someone just punched you in the face) or maybe you feel like you're about to be in an undesirable situation (you're about to make a speech in front of a thousand people and you don't like public speaking)—both of these situations have the same bodily effect, even though one is a tangible threat and one is subjective. These two types of stress are "absolute" stress and "relative" stress.

One of the most cited purposes of stress (or arousal) is that sometimes you need to have all cylinders firing at once to deal with certain threats. The sensation you've evolved to feel when you're all stressed and pumping adrenaline because some troublemaker punched you in the face is the same circuitry that lit up in our ancestors when we were squaring off against some prehistoric predatory threat. Your genes can't distinguish what you're fighting—it just knows you're in trouble. I should say it's more like your genes don't have time to distinguish because the decision to either fight or run away from the threat has to happen fast, as the worst thing to do in a tight situation like that is stand frozen in horror.

So the adrenaline comes out and so does the cortisol—these hormones allow you to do a lot of things that would be useful against a threat to your life. Adrenaline mostly changes the way your body uses its blood so you can be stronger and faster, while cortisol changes the way your body sources its energy and shuts down processes unrelated to the fight. These are handy in certain situations but not things you want happening every second of your normal life. It's essential to be capable of stress, but it's not sustainable. Imagine constantly being in this high-intensity mode—you'd burn yourself to a crisp in no time. It's more like a last resort effort to escape a situation more deadly than the side effects of stress.

Of course, nowadays, encountering deadly beasts is not an everyday occurrence (unless you live in Australia), so what gives? Why do we still get stressed? Well, just like how your stress circuitry can't tell the difference between it being activated to fight off dinosaurs for your ancestors or if you're activating it to fend off random street punks, it also can't tell the difference between if you're fighting a real-life threat or a psychological one. All we're equipped with when it comes to fighting danger is this stress response, so it's what we use, even though we've reached the point in our evolutionary history where most of that danger is emotional.

THE FLASHBULB EFFECT

Stress doesn't just increase our physical capabilities—it's shown to increase our mental capabilities too. To a degree, at least. It's complicated. Well, not *that* complicated, but complicated enough that it has its own dang law.

The Yerkes-Dodson law, named after its creators, psychologists Robert M. Yerkes and John Dillingham Dodson, dictates that you can observe an increase in how well you can do things if you're under more pressure. The arousal that pressure elicits is needed to achieve optimal performance since it can be used in various ways—the extra "power" gained from heightened arousal can be put toward things like boosted concentration or motivation.

An example of how stress can drastically improve one's abilities is the flashbulb effect. People under stress can remember things well when they normally wouldn't. It makes sense that this is the case, since being stressed forces us to open our third eye and pay attention, so we can vividly remember things that happened during those moments since they are better encoded. This can happen without any recollection of the surrounding events at all, and in fact this is kind of the trade-off—details that are irrelevant to the stressful event or that surrounded it chronologically are often forgotten. This is an optimization measure on the part of your brain, since it realizes that if you're having an intense emotional response to something, it should direct your entire attention to that thing. It's called the flashbulb effect after the big lightbulb on old-timey cameras. The vivid but heavily localized memory of the shocking or stressful event is likened to a photograph in its high detail but brief duration. These flashbulb memories can persist in someone's mind for a long time, and that's not surprising considering it sounds like being traumatized.

"Weapon focus" in forensic psychology refers to the tendency for witnesses of violent crimes to vividly remember the weapon used to perpetrate a crime but not much else. This can even include things like forgetting what the person holding the weapon looked like. You'd think that'd be one small part of the larger "photograph" that the witnesses saved in their minds, but it shows how narrow the concentration of memory can get when we feel threatened or shocked.

Of course, all things in moderation—while using stress or arousal to heighten focus to remember things better might sound like a cool way to improve your study sessions, all the regular stuff you know about stress still applies. Chronic stress negatively effects your health in a million and one ways, but even regarding memory, long-term stress can cause the part of your brain that deals with memory to shrink permanently. One of the interesting caveats to the Yerkes-Dodson law is that, while it's true that stress can only make you better at certain tasks (especially things that you know how to do well), the performance boost cuts off and reverses after a certain point when it comes to more complex stuff. So next time you're thinking of cramming hard for a test, remember that constantly using high amounts of stress as your main motivational source is probably not the way to go about things because it's counterproductive—perhaps consider petting a dog from time to time.

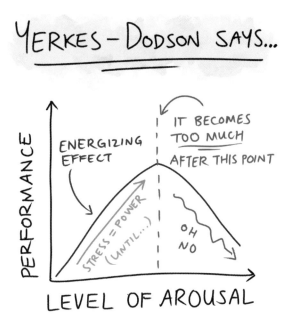

YERKES – DODSON SAYS...

PERFORMANCE

ENERGIZING EFFECT

IT BECOMES TOO MUCH AFTER THIS POINT

STRESS = POWER (UNTIL...)

OH NO

LEVEL OF AROUSAL

IMPAIRED DECISIONS

"Would you always do the same thing
even under different stressors?"

Let's talk about risk. You're bound to make the wrong decision when it comes to strategizing. In this case I mean a work strategy, so your decision to prioritize task A and do it this way instead of task B and doing it that way. Why does it feel so dang hard to get it right sometimes? And even if we get it right, it feels exhausting unless it becomes completely automatic. You won't always have the right answer at your fingertips (unlike when the question is something like, "Should I procrastinate or not procrastinate?")—sometimes the line is blurrier than that. Sometimes, getting started means taking a leap of faith!

So what's the deal on risk? How can we properly assess risk and make the best decisions possible? Well, unfortunately, this book is not a strategy guide for life—you'll have to call the shots on those. What you can take away from this section, though, is knowledge of how we perceive and assess risk. Maybe that knowledge can help you realize where you may be making leaps in logic where you don't want to be and that can inform a decision that leaves you better off! Or maybe you can ignore all of that and bet it all on black. None of this is financial advice. Don't come for me when the boys come a-knockin'.

THE IOWA GAMBLING TASK

Just like how stress has a somatic (bodily) component (hormones), you bet there's a somatic component to assessing and taking risks. Antoine Bechara, Antonio Damasio, Hanna Damasio, and Steven Anderson conducted an experiment in 1994 examining how people respond to gambling tasks. They gave participants of the experiment a computer game where they had to pick cards at random from any of four decks. Selecting a card would either reward or penalize the participant using virtual money and the participants were tasked with getting as much money as possible. They were told that some of the decks had higher rewards than others, but these high-reward decks also had higher penalties. They didn't tell the participants that the riskier decks had horrible odds, mathematically—it was reeeeaaally not worth it to go for the risky deck because the experimenters purposely messed with it to leave people who selected it worse off.

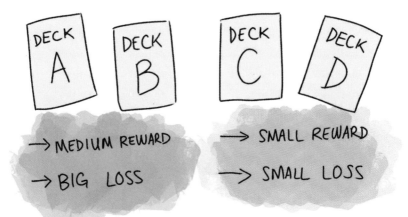

The findings were interesting—the primary discovery being that participants who had damage in the specific section of the brain dedicated to making decisions played significantly differently from people who didn't have this brain damage. The participants who did not have this damage eventually intuitively figured out that the odds were way better if they kept playing the regular, boring deck. It didn't take them that many rounds—in fact, machine analysis showed that their bodies were emitting a stress response when they hovered their cursor over the "bad" deck and this stress response happened even before the participant was aware of the optimal strategy.

The participants with impaired decision-making kept playing the bad decks despite the awful odds and the suboptimal strategy— even while they knew they were using a losing strategy. Interestingly, the participants who engaged in this mode of playing did not show the same stress response from the risky behavior, which offers significant insight into how decision-making, risk assessment, and stress are related.

Making a bad decision or carrying out a poor strategy doesn't mean you have brain damage. Likewise, having impairments doesn't mean you're doomed to always be working sub-optimally. However, it's important to be cognizant of what kind of game you're playing and whether it makes sense to go with the course of action you've chosen from a risk-reward and cost-benefit standpoint. It's easier than you'd think to make weird decisions based on "feel" even if you consider yourself good at strategizing. Take a step back and look at whether you're hurting yourself or others with your choices—you may realize it's time to shift gears.

THE JAM STUDY

You know another thing that clouds our decision-making abilities? The *types* of choices we have in front of us. It's easier to conceptualize risk, reward, success, and failure when it's more mathematical like the Iowa Gambling Task. Even if you're not crunching the exact numbers, the body keeps score in its own way. That's when you're dealing with probabilities and whatnot, but what about when the options and value judgments are more abstract? "One in five chance to win a hundred dollars" contains figures that can be punched into a calculator and therefore can be analyzed at least somewhat objectively.

But what about when you're pondering whether you should eat at a restaurant or go home to cook food? This leads to a calculation that's more wishy-washy and harder to quantify like "low chance that I will be able to make food tastier than what's in the restaurant."

One dimension we often take for granted when it comes to the science of choice is the amount of choices we have in front of us. It's easy to calculate that you should consistently pick the one or two good decks and stay away from the bad decks when you have a small number in front of you. But what if there were a hundred decks? It's not like the process of figuring out which decks are better and worse changes in any huge way—you're eventually gonna find out the optimal strategy after playing long enough. There's a human aspect to this situation that could be missed here, though—the fact that there are a hundred things to choose from might completely throw off everything in our decision-making systems. It doesn't matter that the math doesn't change much; just the scary idea of having a hundred *things* in front of you can easily intimidate you into acting irrationally.

Psychologists Sheena Iyengar and Mark Lepper solidified this idea in the scientific literature with their findings in the now-famous "jam study," wherein they examined how shoppers behave when presented with varying degrees of choice. A display table was set up in a food market that had a bunch of different varieties of jam—either twenty-four or six. The table with twenty-four kinds of jam ultimately sold less than the table with six options—giving evidence that such a thing as "choice paralysis" exists.

Granted, a lot of other studies have tried to replicate, refute, or build upon these findings, but the results of those vary in an interesting way. While the findings were never outright proven false, some experiments showed a lot more nuance to all of this. The specifics of the situation matter when it comes to how likely we are to make certain decisions, which shows that we can't even be aware of how much our strategies are affected by our human nature, no matter how logically or mathematically sound we think they are.

DON'T GET DISTRACTED!

"What?"

This has for sure happened to you at some point—you're writing something down, maybe a greeting on a birthday card or an email for a refund on your life-sized wombat plushie (they are a *lot* bigger than you'd think—one time I saw one in real life and I screamed)—when suddenly, someone asks you a question. Perturbed at the interruption but otherwise happy to answer, you return to writing your thing—only to realize that you accidentally wrote down part of the question that was asked to you. It happens often that people accidentally write down something they hear even if they don't mean to—particularly when they're not especially focused. This is one example of the interesting way our concentration works—sometimes this even works in speech. Surely you've caught someone saying a sentence that didn't make sense because they were thinking about something else while saying it and accidentally said that word.

Believe it or not, even when we think we're in the meat of a nice concentration session, our minds can still wander. You think you're devoting all your energy to something, and yet you can still be diverted off course. We'll look at some famous examples that you might be able to relate to—because who doesn't get distracted from time to time?

DOES MUSIC HELP CONCENTRATION?

Depending on who you ask, music is either a great concentration aid (some people claim they can't work without it!) or a big productivity killer. You don't understand, Mom—I need my tunes! It's not a distraction!

Mom might have a point—in research done by accomplished psychology researchers and professors Manuel F. Gonzalez and John Aiello, the negative effects of music on concentration were found to be...existent. Conditionally.

Before this study, many research results showed that music did have effects on performance—but what *kind* of effect it had varied wildly, with explanations ranging from the music increasing/decreasing attention, affecting the participants' moods, or stimulating them into a higher/lower state of arousal. In their study, Gonzalez and Aiello attempted to contextualize the effects of music by accounting for factors such as the complexity of music, temperament of the individual listening, and the task being performed.

Looking at research that preceded this study, the idea that music would have different effects on task performance based on the context had scientific grounds—Gonzalez and Aiello preface their findings with an acknowledgment of "social facilitation theory"—the tendency for people's task performance level to change depending on the presence or absence of others in the work environment. The execution of "simple tasks" (defined as repetitive, easy-to-learn, or already-known) was significantly helped by having people around, while that of "complex tasks" (defined as new, difficult, or multifaceted) was hampered. The presence of people at all seems to force the brain to allocate resources into accounting for them, even if they just passively exist in the vicinity.

Gonzalez and Aiello had participants complete simple and complex tasks while listening to music. Lo and behold, like with the social facilitation theory, music helped the participants when the task was simple while it hurt their performance when it was complex. This slots into another theory well—the "distraction-conflict theory" describes how simple tasks take less brain power, so they leave more room to let one's mind wander, while complex tasks take more brain power so there is less room for paying attention to other things. If that excess empty brain-wandering space is taken up by music, then you presumably have better concentration since your mind isn't wandering anywhere too distant or deep. On the other hand, having music on while doing a complex task would harm the person's performance since valuable brain real estate is forcefully allocated to attending to the music (since you can't close your ears and block it out).

There's more to this study, with Gonzalez and Aiello also having the participants assess how distractible they were—"distractible" meaning how much they preferred external stimuli to keep them from boredom. Turns out, the people who needed more stimulation suffered more when the music was playing during the complex task. This might sound confusing since you'd think if they need more distraction, they'd welcome the additional stimulus—however, consider that being more susceptible to boredom means you're more susceptible to letting any little thing catch your attention, since you'll do anything not to be bored. Imagine a highly distractible person being told to sit and wait for a long time—they're more likely to tap their leg with their fingers to make a sound to concentrate on or engross themselves in a pattern made by the floor tiles. This comes back to haunt highly distractible people, since even though they're concentrating on a complex task, their mind is still more sensitive to outside distractions like when they weren't doing anything.

It's important to keep in mind that this boredom susceptibility measurement is more akin to a personality-based preference (like how much you like sweet food or how extraverted you are)— so even though these people might say they concentrate better when they turn on music while they work on an essay or study, they're probably wrong.

When doing any task, it's important to realize what obstacles you might encounter, as well as your motivations and tendencies. Of course you can never account for everything, and no doubt you'll make some decisions that yield an undesirable outcome—but that's fine! You're human and that's how humans are supposed to work. That capability to get distracted, become discouraged, make silly mistakes, and get stressed is also the same capability that allows us to achieve so many great things and realize our truest potential. Just don't be too hard on yourself, okay? It's good to have standards but it never helps to be self-critical to the point of being mean.

CHAPTER 3

LIVING IN
A SOCIETY

SOCIAL INFLUENCES

After having read so much blah blah blah about how much we are prone to get swayed by things that aren't in our control, no one would blame you if you began to think more that you're less of a commander of a ship and more like a puppet on a string regarding your perceptions, decisions, and motivations. Things are pulling you every which way and you can't keep track of what and how much!

Well, I've had it with being whipped up in the typhoon of subconscious influence! It's time to flip the narrative! What if we could pull on other people's strings? Can we use the human susceptibility to being influenced to our advantage in social situations? Actually...on that note, how much are we getting pulled on by other people already?

It so happens that we are all pulling on each other's strings simultaneously. This is such a fixture in the sphere of psychology knowledge that you probably already intuitively know some of the phenomena we're going to talk about already, but you never thought about it in terms of scientifically defining it. One example of practical social psychology is advertising: companies will use words, images, logic structures—anything they've got—to influence your perceptions and subsequently your decision-making. Whether you like it or not, you've almost certainly been psychology'd by advertising at some point or another. We'll go into specifics about that in a bit, but the point is that the science of using psychology to get into people's heads for your advantage is an old practice. It's not always a bad thing, nor is it always one-sided. People impacting other people makes society go round. And round and round and round and round and round and round.

Remember the elevator walking speed experiment in Chapter 1? From that you can see how easily someone can make you live in a world of their making. This doesn't mean you're gullible or naive—your brain is doing its best job to react appropriately. It's trying its best to do what anyone else would do—because 99 percent of the time in human history, that's been good enough to keep you alive. Being alive isn't enough to have your genes survive, though—you have to reproduce. Humans being such social creatures means that to pass on genes, you'll have to fit in. So naturally the people that wanted to fit in were mostly the ones who have their DNA in us to this day. That small part of us that resembles those conforming ancestors is the part that makes us feel happy when we're accepted and fit in.

RIDING WITH THE MOB

"All of your friends say root beer is the best soft drink—
are you going to be the weirdo that disagrees?"

"Conformity" is a word you probably know about. It's when we try to stick to what the crowd is doing or what's expected of us. It's similar to obedience, but it doesn't have to be out of dedication to an authority—we want to fit in or blend in. A metric ton of experiments explore the power of conformity, all supremely intriguing and many famous even among people who don't have a vested interest in psychology. Because of how numerous and famous these experiments are, we won't spend too much time on each one to keep this book under six hundred pages. No delay! Let's dive right in!

ASCH CONFORMITY EXPERIMENT

The year is 1951, and Solomon Asch, social psychologist extraordinaire, gets the uncontrollable urge to go ahead and investigate social pressures and the effects of conformity on individuals' behavior. Honestly, relatable. The experiment he chose to conduct involved pressuring an individual to answer questions with statements that are unequivocally false—and you may be thinking, *oh, like make someone lie about what kind of food they like or what they did this morning?* No—present someone with this picture:

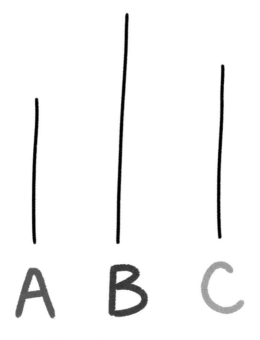

Ask them which line is the longest, and pressure them into saying the one on the right. Heck, sometimes even getting them to say they think the longest is the one on the left. How can someone be convinced to give an answer that is so demonstrably and blatantly wrong?

Well, Asch did it by getting a bunch of actors in the same room as the poor participant getting punked and making the actors confidently put forth wrong answers to all his questions. The details mattered in this experiment—the more actors there were, the stronger the peer pressure, and even one of the actors giving a correct answer made the participants highly unlikely to conform to the majority.

After Asch informed the participants that they were being tricked the entire time, they usually justified their conformity by citing their desire to fit in (to avoid being made fun of or perceived as weird) and their belief that the consensus of the group is more reliable.

MILGRAM'S IRRESISTIBLE OBEDIENCE EXPERIMENT

Chop chop, onto the next conformity experiment! Psychologist Stanley Milgram wanted to investigate how the presence of authority figures influenced behavior. Unlike Asch's experiment, which dealt with what we would call "peer pressure," this is more like "authority pressure" since a power structure is involved.

Milgram tricked participants into thinking they were helping with research into whether punishment helps people learn quickly. He assigned the participants to administer an electric shock to punish someone if they made a mistake in a learning task. These "learners" were actors pretending to be participants and there were no actual electric shocks—they would pretend to be in pain whenever they were "punished." With each subsequent mistake, the participants were tasked to increase the voltage higher and higher, and Milgram found that participants were likely to continue with this cruel behavior if there was an experimenter in the room—i.e., the participants would do something that conflicted with their morals if they felt the pressure of authority. Milgram even had the learners pretend to plead for the shock not to be administered, but many participants carried on anyway—"for the sake of the experiment."

I could've gone with the obvious pun of "Milgram's Shocking Experiment" or "Milgram's Electrifying Experiment," but I went with the infinitesimally less low-hanging fruit joke. Because you're worth it.

SMOKE DETECTOR BYSTANDERS

After the infamous case of Kitty Genovese, a woman murdered in plain sight of numerous witnesses who did not act to aid her, researchers wanted to closely examine the strange behavior of bystanders. John M. Darley and Bibb Latané, social psychologists interested in this "bystander effect" and the psychology behind not taking action in important situations, conducted a famous experiment where they observed what participants would do when they were put in an emergency with strangers. The bystander effect is the broader term for people's tendency to stand there and do nothing in a crowd. It's why, if you're ever in an emergency where you need other people's help, you should single people out and be specific with your requests.

Darley and Latané conducted their bystander effect experiment by putting participants in a room to complete a simple task, instructing them to wait until the experimenter returned if they finished early. The experimenter never returned, however—because they were too busy pumping smoke into the room via air vents to cause alarm in the participants. They found if other people were in the room with them, participants were likely to sit still and not report the smoke or take any action, even if it caused significant discomfort. Have you ever sat in the direct blast zone of a campfire's smoke? Your eyes and nose will not thank you for the experience, I'll tell you that much.

Meanwhile, participants in the room alone were much faster at reacting. Afterward, when asked to justify their inaction, the "group room" participants explained that they figured the smoke wasn't an urgent concern. The general interpretation here is people often look to others around them when gauging the necessity of reaction and the seriousness of the situation.

We are highly context-dependent creatures, huh? We download our surroundings, including others' behavior, faster and harder than we realize. Or maybe we do realize, but we're powerless against the tidal wave that is social obligation. Not like that's a strictly terrible thing, though—it feels nice to fit in. Still, double-checking your moral compass from time to time to make sure you're not getting too lost in the sauce is always helpful, even if it comes at the cost of comfort—so don't go shooting electricity or smoke at people, and don't gaslight them into thinking short lines are long, okay? It's not worth it. They'll think you're weird. You won't be invited to their birthday party.

WITH US OR AGAINST US

"Who can I trust to tell me whom to trust?"

A strong feeling of contentment comes when you have a clear sense of identity—"I fulfill a certain role in this social structure and I fall under this category and that category." Think of all the labels that you can apply to people in this way—"fathers," "teachers,"

"Catholics," "Americans," "Pokémon fans," and so on—all of these can be a part of your identity, even all at once!

When psychologist Henri Tajfel looked into the minimum conditions to make a "group" in 1967, he determined that it didn't take much for people to sort themselves into an identity. He told schoolboys that they belonged to either the "Klee" group or the "Kandinsky" group—these names did not mean anything and there was no significant discerning factor between members of the groups other than the name they were arbitrarily sorted under. He then asked them to rate some abstract paintings, with the only information about the paintings available to them being whether they were "Klee" paintings or "Kandinsky" paintings. Turns out, the boys would give favorable reviews to in-group paintings for no reason other than they were the paintings that belonged to *their* group—all that's needed to create loyalty is the mere existence of a group!

Certain expectations come with labels and we are happy to live up to them—call it a natural human inclination toward "membership." I'm sure you've seen people engage in playful debates about mundane things like "Is GIF pronounced 'ggh-if' or 'jiff'?"—for me, I frequently switch between the two to make people on both sides of the aisle angry on purpose because it's funny.

Defending your stance on little things like this is a microcosm of our tendency to organize other people into "my team" or "the other team." How far does this go, though? Would you make sacrifices if it meant staying dedicated to your identity? Would you hurt other people? Would you act irrationally by all other analyses to preserve the integrity of your membership in a group? You probably get the gist of how the chapters in this book work by now, so let's not delay; it's time to get into what the science says to all of these questions.

THE ROBBER'S CAVE

Meet Muzafer Sherif, who went against his nominal destiny and did not become a sheriff but rather a social psychologist. He wanted to take a closer look at group dynamics, specifically that of rival groups. Like we mentioned before in the GIF pronunciation debate, people tend to not only take sides but seemingly suddenly get along well with people who agree with them on the thing in question. Usually, this kind of debate only arises with those decently familiar with each other, but what would this look like in the context of strangers?

To examine this unique brand of hostility, Sherif had two groups of boys spend their days at a camp. A fun camp, not like a boot camp or something. He had the boys spend time with their campmates, developing in-group customs and named them the Eagles and the Rattlers. The interesting part is, while these mini-cultures were built within the campsites, the two groups were unaware that the other existed.

Sherif then had the two groups encounter each other and subsequently had them participate in competitive games like baseball. Since the games were competitive, structural rivalry was artificially created, but this antagonism extended further than play. Territorialism, unwarranted name-calling, cabin-raiding, even flag-burning ensued—and it was made abundantly clear, without any real order to do so, that the two camps did not think the world of each other. Questionnaires distributed asking about the perception of one's group versus perception of the other group showed, to no surprise, consistent high opinion of one's "society" while showing a high degree of disapproval of the other. Remember the Klees and Kandinskys? This is like that but more *Lord of the Flies*—ish.

Sherif was not about to let the boys walk away forever holding vitriol in their hearts, however—he was also interested in seeing if this conflict could be resolved somehow and if the solution could be extrapolated more generally to create a formula for group conflict resolution. Well, what better way to get people together than to introduce a problem bigger than all of them combined?

The camp had suddenly and mysteriously run out of water one day—which was, of course, a situation engineered by Sherif and his gang. Though the Rattlers and Eagles began their inquiry into the problem's origins separately, they both ended up at the root of the problem—a clogged pipe. The two groups tossed potential solutions and suggestions to each other to achieve the common goal, and in the end, through teeth-clenched teamwork, the boys unblocked the water supply. Surprisingly, even after the problem was fixed, the boys continued being courteous to each other, giving up their spots in line for the drinking water.

The idea that a superseding goal or problem can bring together even the most bitter of rivals hammers home the fact that at the end of the day, the most important group of all is the one that encompasses us as humans. That sounds super hippie and cloyingly idealistic, but we could always use a little more Kumbaya in our lives. Belief in the human spirit and its capacity for compassion and goodwill is one of the greatest pillars of social activity that keeps us afloat, even through cabin-raiding shenanigans and camp-side trifles.

THE STANFORD PRISON
EXPERIMENT

Knowing what group you belong to can solidify your sense of security in your perceptions, but we've seen that it's not always a great thing— what if it causes you to dislike outgroups? What if your sense of identity is tied to some feeling of oppression? What if the role that you play involves making difficult decisions that end up sometimes getting people hurt? Are we to let our morals remain subservient to the requirements of our role? Is it such that perhaps our entire personalities hinge on the responsibilities of our station?

In a famous study called the Stanford Prison Experiment, psychologist Philip Zimbardo examined the effect of the role structure of microsocieties and the expectations that came with certain labels. He had participants split into playing the part of guards or prisoners, complete with costumes and everything. I know what you're thinking: "That sounds so cute. I'd love to do an experiment that lets me cosplay"—you must remember this was in 1971, so the costumes were not cute. He instructed the guards that the only limitations on their actions were that they could not physically abuse the prisoners— but other than that, they were free to go wild in their simulation of prison life.

Immediately, both groups got waaaay into their roles. Imagine the creepy dude in your drama class who says he's a "method actor" as an excuse for being difficult and mean to people backstage when he's playing a villain character. It was that but even wilder. Prisoners started riots against the guards, who in turn had become uncaring and sadistic toward the prisoners. Even Zimbardo realized he thought of himself as a prison superintendent rather than a psychology experimenter. The experiment was cut off less than halfway through and even with its short runtime, showed the world how powerful the effect of role expectations and environment can be.

To this day, the experiment and its findings are plagued with discussion regarding the dubious integrity of its methods and is cited as one of the reasons contemporary psychology experiments have such stringent ethical restrictions, to the point of the experiment being discredited by certain portions of the larger scientific community. Nevertheless, it remains an important part of psychology history and is certainly, at the least, a significant warning against getting lost in the sauce of your position.

AN OFFER I CAN'T REFUSE: BEING PERSUASIVE (EVEN TO ONESELF)

"Can you teach me how to be persuasive? Please?"

Okay, there's a lot of negativity in the air, definitely some sour tastes in the mouths of many after that prison experiment thing. Psychology experiments usually take around an hour to participate in, and even those get tiresome to trudge through, so it's surprising that so many people were willing to sign up for such a convoluted and long experiment. Maybe Zimbardo used some of the psychological persuasion techniques we will talk about and that's how he got so many people on board! Let's go over some great persuasion techniques, starting with:

...yeah, he just paid them. There's your persuasion technique.

DOOR IN THE FACE

Moving on to the next technique, "door in the face" sounds like "foot in the door." "Getting your foot in the door" is an expression that means getting yourself involved in a big situation by first involving yourself in a smaller situation inside that. For example, you can get your foot in the door in the world of food trucks or food carts by becoming friends with a hot dog vendor and asking to watch them do their business for a day. Then you can ask them to show you the ropes—et voilà, you're involved in the exciting world of street food. You put your foot in the door to open it by a crack—then, you reach in with your hand and open it all the way. Turns out, you can also try convincing people to do things this way—you help them get their foot in the door ("Hey, can you pick up my pen for me?") before opening it all the way and asking them for the real big favors ("Since you're holding my pen anyways, can you do my homework for me?").

That probably won't work. It's too big of an ask, and certainly too big of a jump to go from picking up a pen to using it to do someone else's homework. But what if we could use psychology tricks to make it seem like not that big of an ask? Granted, it might not work every time, but maybe we can goose our odds just the slightest bit.

Robert Cialdini, psychologist and professor at Arizona State University, wanted to test how he could adjust people's perspective on requests to make them more likely to comply. Instead of getting their foot in the door with a small request and then slamming them with a big request to follow up, Cialdini reversed the order—he threw open the door in their face with a big, unrealistic request, and then asked them for a small (in comparison) foot-in-the-door level request. A group was asked to volunteer at a juvie prison for two years (a big, big undertaking) before being asked to take the youth at the facility to the zoo for a day. Turns out, a whopping 50 percent of the volunteers agreed to take on the zoo task when asked in this way! This is compared to a measly 17 percent of participants asked only to do the zoo thing without any mention of the two-year volunteer ordeal. Even the suggestion of a bigger thing proved effective—when the two-year volunteering situation was brought up, not even requested, before the zoo request, participants were significantly more likely to agree to the zoo trip.

You can imagine how this technique could extend to marketing. In a concept known as "anchoring," you can change a potential customer's perception of price and savings by introducing them first to a reference point that makes your actual target seem reasonable in comparison. For example, you can make more sales by offering someone something for a hundred dollars before letting them think that they haggled it down to fifty dollars. When you tell them "a hundred dollars," that immediately becomes the starting point for their calculations—by bringing it down by an entire half, you've made them convince themselves that it is cheap since their only point of reference is the big number instead of any smaller numbers.

This works in more convoluted manners too—you can convince someone to purchase a small sticker by asking them to first purchase a huge and cumbersome sticker. They may not have thought of buying the sticker at all, but since their reference point was "gigantic version of the sticker" instead of "nothing," suddenly the idea of walking away having avoided buying a giant and useless sticker at the cost of buying the smaller, fun one that you can at least maybe put on your phone or your diary doesn't sound so bad.

WHEN ONE DOLLAR IS BETTER THAN TWENTY

"I made a wise purchase," you say to yourself after buying a small sticker from a mysterious sticker salesman. "I avoided buying the giant sticker that I couldn't have possibly put anywhere in my house, and instead I obtained this smaller sticker that I can use. Now that I think about it, I always wanted to put some fun stickers on my planner! I'm going to go home and do that right now!"

It's possible that you did plan on buying stickers for your planner and the sticker salesman's sudden appearance from stage right was a fortunate twist of fate for you. However, it's also possible that, if you are not the type of person to use stickers, having made a somewhat irrational purchase has started to have a self-brainwashing effect on you. You automatically begin to convince yourself that you have acted rationally and weren't just suckered into the sale. This is known as self-justification—where, as the name suggests, you try to justify your actions to yourself (even if they conflict with your beliefs) so you're properly convinced that you wanted the circumstances in the first place—or at least that the circumstances aren't as bad as they objectively seem.

Leon Festinger and James Carlsmith were social psychologists interested in how one's opinion might be influenced to change depending on forced or coerced behavior. They had participants carry out very boring tasks that involved little thinking and were mostly just time-consuming motor work. After they were done, they were then paid either one or twenty dollars to introduce and explain the task to the next group of participants who would carry out the tasks. Importantly, they were told to tell the incoming participants that the task was highly worth it. The group that was paid twenty dollars explained the task truthfully since they had no real reason to lie— the main benefit of doing the tasks was that you'd get paid twenty bucks for it. The one-dollar group, meanwhile, had a harder time reconciling that this whole rigmarole was for the greater purpose of one dollar and couldn't buy into the story that the task was worth it for the money—because if they said that, they'd feel like they were lying.

After those initial participants were told to instruct the new batch of people, they were asked to evaluate their enjoyment of the boring tasks. The twenty-dollar group answered truthfully that they didn't enjoy it. The one-dollar group, on the other hand, had more positive things to say about the boring work they were given—they cited that it wasn't so bad and was mildly entertaining. What's going on here? The one-dollar group doesn't need to lie; the experiment is over, right? Well, it's not that they're lying per se—between the time that they had to make up a story in their heads about why the boring tasks are great and when they were asked how enjoyable the tasks were, the fact that they were compensated only one dollar subconsciously drove them to make up a narrative that allowed them to not feel uncomfortable about the disparity between the difficulty of the task and the reward. The disparity could be made up by the fact that they had fun doing it! So there!

This study outlines another significant concept in psychology called cognitive dissonance, which you may have heard as a term thrown about here and there, but we'll get to that later. Stay tuned! It's cool! It's not what you think it is! Or maybe it is! Guess you'll have to read on to find out! I love exclamation points!

SO LONG, SUCKERS!

"Who needs friends anyway?"

All this talk about social pressures, roles, persuading, and whatnot have something in common—they're all somewhat of a two-way street. As much as we conform to the crowd, we are also part of the crowd that exerts pressure. We like to make ourselves part of a group, and in doing so we further define the group's identity. Social interaction, direct or indirect, almost always has to consider that everything is happening under a sort of social script. However, what about selfishness? Selfishness is the spanner in the works regarding social interaction—it's not something that's "supposed" to be accounted for in calculating outcomes regarding interaction because you assume everyone will act within reason.

You give the hot dog cart vendor your money because you expect that, soon after, they will give you a hot dog for it. Of course, checks and balances are in place—for example, if they don't give you the hot dog, their reputation will take a severe hit. And, usually it's hard to run away when you're at a hot dog cart so you can probably assume that you'd have the upper hand in an altercation if you had to start throwing hands to get your hot dog. Other things factor into the trust you have for this hot dog stranger, of course—you might have seen that they made a sale without any issue for the person in front of you, you may not have heard of any hot dog vendors stealing money from their customers, or you may have reasoned out in your mind that no rational person would risk the social, physical, and legal fallout of stealing a hot dog's worth of money.

So what's the point of being selfish? Well, when the conditions are right, sometimes it's easy to think that, all things considered, the best course of action is to be selfish. Whether it saves you time, money, or effort, even the most rational and civilized of people can act in their immediate interest at the expense of others from time to time.

Considering this, the question should be more like: "Why would *anyone* ever *not* be selfish?"—because after all, the "warm fuzzy feeling" of being a nice person can only carry your behavior so far, right? Let's look at this question further—in the lab!

"The Good Samaritan" is the name of a famous parable in the Bible, where a man gets attacked by thieves and left for dead on the side of a road. A priest happens upon him and decides that he can't help the dude. Whether it's because he thought it was not worth the effort or maybe he got too nervous to act (kind of like the phenomenon we discussed in the bystander effect), we don't know. Later, one of the guy's countrymen passes by and he, too, avoids him without helping out. Finally, a Samaritan (Samaritans being a group with strained relations with the Jews at the time) discovers him and immediately pulls out all the stops to help—clothing him, housing him, giving him money, and the works. Pretty swell guy!

While we can't immediately say that the two people that passed the victim are selfish, we can say the Samaritan was the most selfless person in this story, and he acted this way without any tangible benefit to himself. And if you had to categorize the action of not helping a dying man into either selfish or non-selfish, you'd probably end up putting it in the "selfish" bin. Considering all this, do you think you're selfish? Would you have helped the man?

Well, it's likely you may not have—at least, that's what the findings of social psychologists Daniel Batson and John M. Darley say. Bonus points if you recognize Darley—this is his second mention in the book. You go, J.D.

In 1973, Darley and Batson wanted to see if people were more motivated to help based on the goodness of their hearts or whether it was largely influenced by circumstance. The study participants, students aspiring to become religious leaders, were told to prepare a speech to be presented in a different building. They were divided into three groups: participants who were told they would be early to give the speech if they left the building now, those who were told they would be on time, and those who were told they were already late. On the way to the other building, they would each encounter a stranger (an actor!) who had fallen on the floor and was visibly distressed—clearly, they needed help.

Turns out the parable was statistically accurate, all things considered—only 40 percent of the participants offered any help to the fallen stranger. 63 percent of the early group, 45 percent of the punctual group, and 10 percent of the late group gave the stranger their attention—ironically, one of the speech prompts was about the story of the Good Samaritan.

The study then dug deep into the religious influence aspect of things, but we'll spare you the details from here. And listen, we're not making any value judgments on whether we want you to be a certain way in the context of this Good Samaritan situation—but while we don't want to be a nagging mom or nagging priest or nagging video game tutorial NPC, we want to emphasize it would be a beautiful world to live in where we all act in the interest of helping our neighbors. This is a long way of saying please stop putting your feet up on the seat next to you on the bus during rush hour; I keep bumping into people and just want to sit.

THE SELFISH ARGUMENT FOR SELFLESSNESS

Are we doomed by our nature and circumstances to be selfish all the time? How can anyone find the time to be selfless in this busy modern world? You're lying on the side of the road, injured and mugged, and you need me to help dress your wounds and report the incident to the authorities? Well, I'll see if I can pencil that in between my four o'clock shareholders meeting and my six o'clock group rooftop flying yoga lessons (it gets expensed from the company budget).

For legal reasons I have to inform you that that was not an actual, indictable statement of something I (or anybody I know) do, but it is demonstrative of the mindset that some people can easily believe is the prevailing attitude toward the idea of altruism these days. It's easy to believe the world is getting more "all about me, me, me" every day, as we feel like no one's on our side and no one would have any reason to be. After all, what's the point of helping others if it's just going to come at a cost to you?

Let me cap this section with more scientifically salient grounds for prosocial behavior. It's often been observed in bird populations that cooperation gets individuals further in the long term than selfish action. This can encompass minor things, like not reciprocating back scratches (since birds can't scratch and groom their own backs, they get their friends to do it before returning the favor). The social ostracization incurred by self-serving behavior is already enough to filter out an individual's DNA from the gene pool, but sometimes it goes deeper than that. While birds are a departure from psychology, the fact that we can contextualize their behavior in human terms means the example isn't so far off from our lived reality as it might seem. This research provides important context to untangle mysteries in our evolutionary psychology and the history of our behavior from when we were closer to our animalistic ancestors than our current-day iterations.

Countless studies of birds have shown cooperation is a wickedly effective strategy to survive through harsh conditions, and this is also true when the individual birds teaming up aren't blood-related. Often, birds help raise chicks that aren't theirs when times are tough (lack of food or water, bad weather, etc.). It does the species a great deal of good to do this—combining efforts to keep everyone going ensures everyone gets their fair share of what can be achieved when many hands are put to the task. It should be said that cooperating birds don't have a significant advantage over selfish ones when times are plentiful and nice, though. This is all analogous to what we see in our human societies—there's only room for selfish behavior in times of prosperity, but when the pedal hits the metal and it comes down to it, the selfless players win the game.

DEBUNKED!

It's time for a psychology myth lightning round—a rapid-fire list of false "facts" that have made their rounds without having the science to back them up.

Myth: "People only use 10 percent of their brain."

Fact: One look at a brain scan tells you that the entire brain is being used even while resting.

Myth: "Group brainstorming increases productivity."

Fact: Studies show that having too many team meetings can impede progress on an assignment, as it eats up time and decreases the quality of ideas.

Myth: "Nice guys finish last."

Fact: Women aren't generally attracted to "bad boys"— they're shown to be more attracted to kindness and loyalty.

Myth: "Listening to classical music makes babies smarter."

Fact: Nah—while music itself has innate benefits, nothing about music that is specifically classical is shown to have much of an effect on cognition.

Myth: "Attention deficit hyperactivity disorder (ADHD) manifests in people who are misbehaved or were raised incorrectly."

Fact: ADHD has a large genetic component and is too complex to be decisively caused by one thing.

Myth: "Playing hard-to-get makes you more attractive."

Fact: No. Don't do this. It makes you more unattractive, scientifically speaking. And it's inconsiderate!

Myth: "Humans are naturally selfish."

Fact: Sharing can be taught and encouraged in children, but they've been shown to inherently have a grasp on the concept and are naturally inclined to help others.

Myth: "You are either more right-brained or more left-brained."

Fact: The different halves of the brain carry out different functions, but your personality isn't dominated or determined by this.

Myth: "You have to be a perfect match to be perfect friends."

Fact: Disagreement between two people is shown to create deeper understanding and good friendships.

Myth: "It's easy to convince people by using their emotions."

Fact: It's been shown that using emotional appeals such as fear or pity are less effective than logical arguments on complex issues.

Myth: "Lie detectors detect lies."

Fact: What we commonly think of as "lie detectors" are flawed and are subject to influence from things like human error and emotional context.

CHAPTER 4

WHAT'S IN
AN OPINION?

BELIEFS, ATTITUDES,
LIKES, AND DISLIKES

Do you like waffles? Who's the coolest movie character? What's your least favorite trait in other people? After seeing how much we are subject to the whims and fancies of other people in the last section, it's easy to see how much it matters what the opinions of the people around us are. Having an opinion is generally good, since it means you have a decently well-thought-out structure of how things are or ought to be. There are caveats to this; an uninformed or heavily biased opinion might lead you to make judgments that aren't fair or wise. What if you thought you hated eating oranges until you realized you're supposed to peel them before biting in? There are people like this. Not naming names.

Keeping yourself vague and not forming any opinions is akin to letting yourself get whipped into any which way by a whirlwind—you don't have a destination and you're certainly not going to find yourself in a good place often. We like to think that our individual personalities have a large effect on our personalities—after all, if you're a neat freak, for example, you'd probably prefer clean food like steak rather than messy food like barbecue ribs. But what does the juicy psychology research say about all this? How much are human opinions influenced by little idiosyncrasies in our cognitions? What if the opinions we think we're forming based on experience, sensations, logical theory, or personality are forming due to how our brains are structured?

Remember when we talked about cognitive dissonance in Chapter 3? Did you skip ahead to this part? I won't be upset. I promise. Just tell the truth. Did you? If you did, it's okay because I will formally introduce the idea now: cognitive dissonance is when one's actions go against their beliefs. For example, there's an innate cognitive dissonance between people who say they are animal lovers while also eating meat. That's not a moral criticism or anything—it's just that logically, one would assume at first glance that those two things are incommensurate. Of course, then you get into the nitty-gritty details and find the nuance and justification that goes into it ("I like animals like dogs and cats, not farm animals!" "I do love animals and wish I could stop eating meat, but it's just too tasty"). There's an inherent balance being calculated within the person's head, and the calculation itself is not nearly as objective as one would think.

Perhaps when calculating the balance between "being an animal lover" and "eating meat," the person might tip the balance in their favor by purposely avoiding looking at any pictures or videos of animals typically used for food production. Maybe they purposely try not to bring to mind the image of the animal when making food purchases. Maybe they had an opportunity to watch a documentary about big corporate meat industry practices but chose not to so they could stay in the dark about it. The point is, even if this isn't a conscious effort, this kind of thing happens on its own to a lot of people.

ME & THE BESTIES!

What's going on? Did you feel uncomfortable while reading that? It could be because you felt personally called out. I know I kinda did. If you're feeling greatly uncomfortable, it could be because of the forced attention on the dissonance itself. One of the key, most practical bits of knowledge on cognitive dissonance is that the bigger the gap between the two incompatible beliefs, the more discomfort it will cause in the individual that holds them. People typically deal with this discomfort by either avoiding it (like how some people try to ignore the meat documentaries) or by taking action to close the gap (like how some people go vegetarian... or I guess the alternative is to declare you're not so much of an animal lover after all).

A practical example of this is in self-discrepancy theory, which outlines how dissonance in self-image affects people's mood and motivation. According to self-discrepancy theory, you cast an ideal image of yourself in your head—your "ought" self. As in, the you that you "ought" to be—the dream goal self that you want to achieve. However, on Earth, there is the "actual" self. This is you, according to how you judge yourself. The further away your actual and ought selves are, the greater the effects of self-discrepancy-induced discomfort.

The whole point of this self-discrepancy and cognitive dissonance is that your opinions don't have to make "sense" through logical analysis—they just happen. You're not forming opinions from the ground up; it's more like you get opinions thrust onto you and then you tack on an evaluation of whether they're justified. It's a big, tangled mess of opinions that you build up throughout your life and you'd rarely take the time to clean up the ones that don't match—so yeah, you can plausibly be sitting on the idea that you like relaxing and being lazy while simultaneously sitting on the dream of being a hard-working student and industrious member of society. That's how opinions work.

PERSONAL TASTE

"Do I like the things I like,
or do I like the things around them?"

Going out to dinner with friends is a good experience. There's good food, it's a lot of fun talking to your buds, and you get to learn about the culinary scene in the area. But wait a minute—eating out at a restaurant is expensive, loud, time-consuming, and risky since there's a chance I won't like the kind of food they serve. I don't like eating out at restaurants; I like the atmosphere it provides for hanging out with friends.

Without that secondary analysis, it'd have been easy for me to say that yeah, I like going out to eat. Only upon further thought do I realize maybe it's not the restaurant that informs that opinion. This is just an example, of course, of how one can trick themselves into fully believing they like something for reasons that are secondary to the actual thing. It's an example and not an actual scenario because I don't have any friends to go to restaurants with. Now while it's easy to imagine this kind of internal mix-up happening between liking restaurants and liking friends, what if your opinions could be influenced by things that are completely irrelevant?

HALO EFFECT

Professors Karen Dion, Ellen Berscheid, and Elaine Hatfield were greatly interested in how people formed positive opinions of others. Berscheid and Hatfield are especially famous in social psychology for their work on the theory of love. This work on love and attraction informed inquiry into how attraction could warp people's perspectives and thus their opinions. It's time to address the question of the hour—is there such a thing as "hot person privilege"?

The trio conducted an experiment, now well-known amongst people who aren't educated in psychology, investigating whether a person's looks could affect how their personality is interpreted. The experimenters gave volunteer participants photos of people at one of three different levels of attractiveness—"attractive," "average," and "unattractive." They were then asked to guess their personality traits, happiness, future success, and career paths by looking at them.

Participants gave more favorable judgments to the attractive people, saying they probably had more positive traits, were happier, and were more capable. It's as if their attractiveness cast a ring of light around them, illuminating their other traits like their personality or competence—hence the phenomenon being dubbed the "halo effect"! What's the overall conclusion? If you want to pretend you're good at something, make sure you look good while you're doing it.

SUPERFLUOUS APOLOGY

Sorry about how long that word is. "Superfluous" means "excessive" or "overkill." Do you remember the first line of the first page of this book? We talked about how you might be more inclined to keep reading after seeing a random apology, even if it didn't make sense. That's exactly what the research by Alison Wood Brooks,

Hengchen Dai, and Maurice E. Schweitzer investigated as they sought to document the effects of saying "sorry" on being seen as more trustworthy.

They had a confederate (another word for an experiment assistant) go to a train station and ask random people if he could borrow their phone. The confederate was not made aware of the hypothesis and simply approached the randos in one of two ways: saying either, "I'm so sorry about the rain! Can I borrow your cell phone?" or "Can I borrow your cell phone?" While not even 10 percent of people handed over their phone if there was no apology, almost half of the people who had heard an apology ended up agreeing to lend it. Note that apologizing to a stranger for rain does not inherently demand responsibility from the person apologizing—you can't control the weather, so why apologize? Turns out, it doesn't matter—the fact that there is a "sorry" at all is all it takes to increase trust.

There were a bunch of other experiments conducted in the same study that looked for the same thing, but the rain one is the most famous. This is something that you might see backfire in the modern day—whenever celebrities or influencers make apology videos or statements when it turns out that they did something wrong, a common criticism is that they often apologize for the sake of apologizing and don't acknowledge what they did. Also, other research suggests that apologizing might sometimes make people perceive you as weak—so be intentional and responsible when you're throwing out your apologies! Or else the dogs will be barking at your door.

FAMILIARITY BREEDS CONTEMPT

"Go with what you know or explore if there's more?"

Sitting on a sofa on a lazy Sunday morning, you have the sudden urge to watch a movie. You open the movie catalog and scroll through...and scroll through...and keep scrolling through...

It's now Monday, you still want to watch the movie. You are still scrolling through the catalog when suddenly you happen upon it—that one movie you've watched 700 billion times. You've memorized every line, every scene, the timing on each eye twitch and footstep. You are drawn in once more to the alluring light of your comfort movie. You press play. Here we go again.

Oh yeah, this movie's the best. You love the main character (or the secondary main character, or the villain, or whatever)—in fact, you downloaded their entire personality because they're so cool and you want to be like them. In so many ways, this movie has changed who you are. This isn't an uncommon practice though—any time you watch a movie anywhere, you download the personality of the coolest character so you can like yourself more.

But how are you ever going to be your own person this way? One day, you will have to face the world, and you'll be in a situation that didn't appear in the movie. Where's the impetus for learning, for development, for improvement? Do I have to find it somewhere else? Does this copying of characters make you unoriginal? Well, no! At least, I hope so. Because I do that too. Believe it or not, it's a described phenomenon (sort of)—and a viable way to encourage personal growth.

You want personal growth, right?

SELF-EXPANSION MODEL

First proposed by professor of psychology Arthur Aron, the self-expansion model is a theory that people inherently have the urge to integrate bits and pieces of the people around them (the good bits and pieces, not the stinky ones) while improving their relationships with these people. This is presumably rooted in the desire to feel competent—something like: "If I copy people I admire, that means I'm more likely to be good at the things they're good at!" This recombinant self is reiterated again and again with a growing list of constituent parties to make the individual something more than what they started as—and perhaps that's what it means to grow as a person with the help of others.

To illustrate the point, John M. Malouff and Kimberley Coulter's research into the self-expansion model found that it could be applied to couples to improve their relationships. They provided a hundred couples with a four-week "relationship excitement program" where exciting activity ideas were given and encouraged to be participated in for ninety minutes a week.

They found that couples who participated in the study showed higher-than-average levels of satisfaction and excitement in their relationships, even several months after the study finished. The same old date, location, and activities might make a relationship stale and in fact, unfortunately, might increase the chance of one party being unfaithful. With a simple investment of barely over an hour a week, however, couples who put themselves out there and allowed themselves to absorb new aspects of their personalities, together, were all the better for it.

Change doesn't have to be dramatic or stressful—it can be fun, exciting, or relaxing—the point is, exploring what's out there is the only way to expand your horizons. That goes for self-improvement, relationship integrity, and yes, taste in movies.

WHO'S WITH ME ON THIS?

"Is the only person you're convincing...yourself?"

Hey folks, I know we're all thinking it, but I'll be the first to say it—you've got to admit that banging your shin on furniture doesn't hurt; we react like it does because it's the socially acceptable thing. Right? If you think about it, that's what's going on. Right? ...right?

This is something that I've heard someone say with my actual ears and had them repeat and put into writing because I could not believe how far off an experience this was to the vast majority of human beings that have ever lived. What kind of crazy person doesn't let out a small tear when they viciously smash their shin into the side of a table or sofa? It will never be known to mankind or its successors what exactly inspired the confidence to say this, but, in any case, the interesting part is that the person saying it thought that everyone else would agree with it. In fact, more interestingly, they thought they were all *secretly* experiencing the same thing—this means they came to this conclusion without even having seen anyone else act in a manner that would indicate they'd agree.

The phenomenon of thinking something is relatable only to be catastrophically wrong is universally well-documented and, like everything in this book, has its own "effect" name:

FALSE CONSENSUS EFFECT

To put that phenomenon into more science-y terms, there seems to be a bias in people's assumptions about the commonality of their habits, values, and behavior with others. To examine this further, Lee Ross, David Greene, and Pamela House of Stanford University conducted several studies, all showing the fun ways that people inflate the ubiquity of their beliefs. One experiment was dubbed the "supermarket story" since it happened at a supermarket. And it was a story.

Participants in the experiment were given an open-ended story where they went to a supermarket and, upon exiting, were asked by a stranger whether they liked the supermarket. After responding that they liked the store and listing the reasons why, the stranger reveals that, bro, the camera's right there!—they were being filmed the entire time and would like to use their testimony in a commercial. At this point, the participants were asked how many of the other participants would agree and how many would disagree, before also being asked their choice. Real quick, why don't you try for yourself—which would you choose, and how many people would probably agree with you?

Well, the "We're all thinking it!" bias struck again—each side of the decision rated their choice as being the probable popular choice among the public. Did you do that as well? Maybe you purposely did it the opposite way since you saw where this was going. Boo, no fun.

BELIEF PERSEVERANCE

We've all learned by now that it's okay to be on the wrong side of the argument or the data—it might not feel good to admit it, but it's okay. Well, turns out that despite this irrefutable fact of life, we're programmed to avoid being wrong anyway. Obviously you can't **choose** never to get anything wrong; your knowledge limits that. You **can** initiate some sick, crazy mental gymnastics to find some loophole to avoid acknowledging you are wrong when faced with evidence. Often, you'll see people clearly in the wrong bring up weird, non-important details or lie when presented with something that goes against their beliefs. This is the default setting for people, as a matter of fact—it's not that they are intentionally trying to be difficult.

"Belief perseverance" is the tendency for people to hold on to something they believe even when evidence is put forth that they could be incorrect or should change their opinion. Remember the meat-eaters in the cognitive dissonance example we talked about earlier in the chapter? Maybe if they watched that meat industry documentary, they'd still hold on to their affinity for meat. You'll often see it stated that conspiracy theorists will latch on to their beliefs harder when presented with counterevidence— it's hard to win in this type of argument, so it's often a better idea not to bother. For your sake.

If somebody asks you what belief perseverance is and the only example you can think of offhand is conspiracy theorists, you might get some eye rolls for being too political or too edgy, so I'll provide a nice, science-y experiment that's sure to go over well with most people. This study was done by Elizabeth S. Sechler, who assigned participants to write a justification for one of two hypotheses: "Risky people make better firefighters" or "Conservative people make better firefighters." It's important to note that she didn't ask them for their opinion on the issue of what personality is more desirable in firefighters—she assigned them the conclusion and made them extrapolate on it afterward.

In essence, the participants were being induced into having a certain informed opinion. The fun part came afterward, when they were then shown various profiles of firefighters, which included their personalities and performance—with the profiles sometimes showing a combination of personality and performance that directly went against the hypothesis that the participant worked on. Despite tangible proof that they could be wrong, participants interviewed afterward were shown to keep the opinion they fought for during the experiment. It could be that the security found in nestling into a certain worldview is too much to cast away in the face of damning information—they'd rather live in denial than have to create a new bed to lie in.

EVERYONE'S AN IDIOT EXCEPT FOR ME!

*"Does being the only normal one
make you the weird one?"*

You're not all that. Sorry, but it's true! It's okay though—no one is. Except for Leonardo da Vinci. That guy was the definition of "all that." They made a name for people like him who were good at everything: "polymath," which is Greek for something approximating "this guy is *all that.*"

Now I'm sure you're a lovely person and you're wonderful and capable in many ways. Maybe you're better than da Vinci! That'd be awesome to have a person like that around. The real reason we open the chapter like that is to establish a human universal— that is, we make mistakes. You saw as much in the previous section with the firefighters. Sometimes you can be wrong and not know it! But what about being morally or socially wrong?

Take the title of this section, for example—"everybody's an idiot except for me"; that is a presumptuous claim, but it's probably something you've heard someone say unironically, at least indirectly. Setting aside the unlikeliness that you'd happen to find yourself so intellectually superior to every person around you to the point that it warrants complaining, it's kind of a mean thing to say. It's more likely that the person saying this is the one that has blind spots that need addressing and maybe they are causing more problems long-term. If you haven't met somebody this insufferable in your life before, you are one blessed individual. Let's dive right in on what the research says about someone who might think something like this.

THE DUNNING-KRUGER EFFECT

No way we would write a psychology book full of science-y effects and not mention this one. Getting tired of that one person who keeps boasting about how awesome they are and putting others down because they think they're better than everyone else? Well, maybe they're subject to the Dunning-Kruger effect. Named after social psychologists David Dunning and Justin Kruger, this cognitive bias causes incompetent people to believe they are more competent than they are. The case for this is intuitive—people who lack the knowledge or skill to properly assess competence would also be bad at judging their performance properly.

Now while Dunning and Kruger did multiple studies in different domains of competence, we'll look at the domain of humor because being funny is something I wish I was competent at.

In advance of their experiment on competence versus self-assessment of competence, the experimenters had a bunch of professional comedians rate several jokes from a list based on how funny they were. Universally, funny jokes were labeled as funny and non-funny jokes were labeled as such, showing that there was some level of shared expertise among the comedians.

They then had a group of students give ratings to the jokes. Maybe you see where this is going? The students were then asked what they thought of their predicted performance in this domain—so whether they thought they were good at identifying good humor. Oh yeah, you see where this is going. Turns out, the students the worst at rating funniness accurately also consistently rated themselves within the top half of all participants. Yikes. You ever seen someone confidently shout a joke that does not bang, and the situation becomes super awkward? Maybe this is where that comes from.

You have to feel bad for these people who make inflated self-assessments. In a beautiful quote from the study,

"Not only do these people reach erroneous conclusions and make unfortunate choices, but their incompetence robs them of the metacognitive ability to realize it."

—David Dunning and Justin Kruger

Dunning and Kruger went right for the throat on that one.

INSECURITY AND PROJECTION

Have you ever opened up to someone about a problem you're having and then the other person starts giving weirdly specific, unsolicited advice that doesn't have to do with your problem?

Yeah, it's clear that Pink Psi over there is the one with the video game problem and they might be a little insecure about it, not Blue Psi. Pink Psi is projecting—they're casting their image onto the person they're talking to, regardless of whether the person actually shares those traits.

For a long time, projection was a psychological idea associated with other Freudian misconceptions and not necessarily grounded in any clinical science, or at least none that had any measurable results. That is until social psychologists Leonard Newman, Kimberley J. Duff, and Roy F. Baumeister examined this in a laboratory setting and established a model that could be supported by empirical evidence.

If someone is insecure about something, they will actively try to avoid associating themselves with that quality. For example, maybe you don't want to believe you're a control freak. This makes it so that every time you're faced with the possibility of having to consider that a possibility, you actively suppress the thought. While that works out conveniently in everyday life, it also makes it so that there's a "control freak"–shaped hole constantly somewhere deep in your mind. Then, when you see someone behave in a way that kind of fits into that hole, you're immediately more likely to access the descriptor of "control freak" to describe them. And of course, since it's something you don't want to be, it's something you make sure everybody knows bothers you.

Newman, Duff, and Baumeister had a bunch of people fill in some questionnaires that, upon analysis, let them know whether the person who filled it out was repressing negative aspects about themselves as well as what those aspects were. Those repressing themselves were called "repressors" and their associated unwanted negative trait was called the "threatening trait."

They then ran an experiment where participants were given a situation to judge. The situations were made-up stories written in a way that could be interpreted in several ways, such as a story of a man who declines to help his neighbors with a task because he made plans with his family. The participants were asked to interpret the behavior, specifically attributing a quality to the main character in the story. Now with a story like that, you can see it in two ways: a positive way, where the man is loyal and family-oriented, or a negative way, where the man is being selfish. The results showed that people with "selfishness" as their threatening trait were far more likely to have a bad impression of the man in the story and call him selfish. He was trying to keep his family happy!

They conducted several other studies in addition to this, but the general findings remained consistent—people feel disturbed by traits they're trying to avoid, but this practice of avoidance leaves the trait more accessible. I'd better make sure I don't meet anyone insecure about being standoffish, in case they interpret my social withdrawal as such.

CHAPTER 5

LOOKING INTO THE HEART

LOVE, DEVELOPMENT, AND RELATIONSHIPS

If you ask someone for a practical application of psychology knowledge, it won't be long before that someone probably produces an answer alluding to its utility in navigating personal relationships. Now this is a little different than the societal influences we examined in that other chapter with the social pressures and persuasion stuff—right now, we're dealing more with matters of the heart. The real meat and bones of interaction—relationships!

Relationships aren't a zero-sum game. You'll never extract as much benefit from a relationship as you contribute, whether that's because you're extracting more than you contribute or the other way around. To break down relationships into this arithmetic is suspect—you'd think that in all the things to not put under a microscope too harshly, up there should be our connections with the people among us. We don't want to sabotage our bond with others by obsessing over keeping everything calculated and accounted for, like some sort of artificial intelligence impostor-human, but it's also true that relying too much on intuition and feeling with a lack of knowledge about relationships could cause us to lose sight of what is good for us and what isn't. You don't want to catch yourself venting at an inappropriate time, end up accidentally hurting someone, or fail to realize when you should eject yourself from a relationship. A relationship is only as good as its crewmates, after all.

Though you can never get it perfectly balanced, as all things should be, it's important to try to maintain a balance in how much you give and how much you receive.

Human relationships aren't "solved" by any means, and while the intentions of the studies in this section may be something proximal to reaching that "solved" state, the presentation of relationship research in this book is not an attempt to minimize your lived experience! It's just fun trivia context for that crazy thing we call love.

WHAT A BABY WANTS

"What does 'mother' mean to an infant?"

A child's first "real" interaction, with rare exceptions, is with their caregivers. Maybe some older siblings are in the mix. Maybe a crime-solving, talking squirrel is also present. In contrast with humans, there are, of course, animals that don't hang with their kids—turtles, fish, and crabs, for example, are usually dipping out shortly after laying their eggs. Their propagation strategy is more like "have lots of eggs and hope a good portion of them survive" rather than "have a small number of offspring and care for them super vigilantly." Turtles, fish, and crabs all start ready to function—you've probably seen a depiction of the famous turtle exodus in media, where baby turtles immediately make a mad dash for the water after they are born on the beach sands. Humans, on the other hand, are born useless—we can't do anything. We are extremely vulnerable and not ready to make any complex motor actions like running, let alone running in a specific direction at high speed.

It makes sense, then, that we are so attuned and ready to commit so much to our babies: resources, time, affection—because if we had evolved to be any different, those babies would not be making it out the other side in nearly as good shape. Perhaps our hypersensitivity to emotion, something that we highly associate with what it means to be human, has some of its roots deeply entrenched in this baby framework. Whether they're holdovers from when we were babies or ammo to prepare us to care for one, our emotions are the guiding principle on which our caregiving and care-receiving behavior operates.

Crabs are demonstrably less emotional than people.

Not everyone will have a kid, and not everyone has their parents—that's okay. In the present day, the parent-child–focused biological architecture remains within us since most of our relevant evolutionary history has been oriented toward this dynamic, even though it may not be exactly "relevant" in a relatable way to some people. To investigate the origins and intricacies of our developmental emotional needs and the process behind them, the research surrounding those should be in a setting that resembles the primordial condition—which is why the science we will look at regards family dynamics and the science of attachment through the medium of the common mother-child dyad.

FAMILY PICTURE

THE STRANGE SITUATION

Babies are a basket of fun. And a basket full of babies would be an exponential basket of fun! Unfortunately, no baskets are mentioned in the report of this next experiment, but there are some babies, which is awesome. Developmental psychologist Mary Ainsworth wanted to look into attachment styles—that is, how a person's nature would affect their behavior in domains such as exploration, separation, how they deal with strangers, and so on. You may have heard of "attachment styles" already, and their fame could be traced back, at least in part, to this study. Ainsworth wanted to examine how attachment styles manifest and develop during infancy.

To back up a little, what we know now as "attachment styles" is how we interpret and express intimacy and closeness and is thought to stem from how we bond with our caregivers during early life. The four attachment styles identified in adults are commonly cited as being "avoidant," "fearful-avoidant," "anxious," and "secure." These are self-explanatory, but their definitions are:

- **Avoidant:** Often associated with being emotionally unavailable or being uninterested or afraid of intimacy.

- **Fearful-avoidant:** A strange, uncommon attachment style marked by craving affection but also fear of getting close.

- **Anxious:** The typical "clingy" attachment style—fearing abandonment.

- **Secure:** A balanced attachment style that appreciates company and knows how to trust others without being too dependent.

While this is the elaborated attachment theory we know today, at the time of Ainsworth's study this idea was still in its infancy (pun intended). In fact, one of the main takeaways from the study itself was the solidification of these classifications!

Ainsworth had infants go through eight engineered scenarios over twenty minutes. They were as follows:

1. The mother and baby are introduced to the experiment room (new place)

2. The baby is allowed to explore while the mom watches (exploration)

3. A random person enters the room, interacting with mother and baby (new person)

4. The mother leaves the room and the stranger attends to the baby (learning to trust)

5. The mother comes back as the stranger leaves and plays with the baby (reunion)

6. The mother leaves the room again (separation)

7. The stranger enters the room (trusted person)

8. The mother comes back and the stranger leaves (second reunion)

You don't need to memorize that. The important part you need to know is that it can be condensed down to the following:

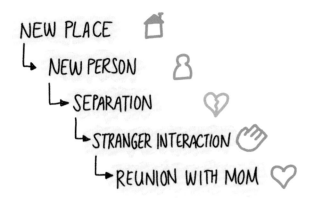

NEW PLACE
↳ NEW PERSON
    ↳ SEPARATION
        ↳ STRANGER INTERACTION
            ↳ REUNION WITH MOM

From the baby's behaviors during these stages, Ainsworth identified what are now like the granddaddies of the modern attachment styles—"secure attachment," "resistant attachment," and "avoidant attachment." "Resistant" in this case is equivalent to today's anxious attachment. Here's how they distilled the behavior of the kids to place them into their respective categories:

SECURE KIDS

NEW PLACE { CHILLING, EXPLORING
↳ NEW PERSON { IS OKAY IF MOM IS THERE
  ↳ SEPARATION { SAD...
    ↳ STRANGER INTERACTION { KINDA SPOOKED
      ↳ REUNION WITH MOM { HAPPY!

RESISTANT (AKA ANXIOUS) KIDS

NEW PLACE { NOT INTO EXPLORING
↳ NEW PERSON { SPOOKED
  ↳ SEPARATION { BIG SAD
    ↳ STRANGER INTERACTION { VERY SPOOKED
      ↳ REUNION WITH MOM { MAD AT MOM FOR LEAVING

AVOIDANT KIDS

NEW PLACE { CHILLING, EXPLORING
↳ NEW PERSON { DOESN'T CARE
  ↳ SEPARATION { DOESN'T CARE
    ↳ STRANGER INTERACTION { TREATS STRANGER & MOM EQUALLY
      ↳ REUNION WITH MOM { DOESN'T CARE

When accounting for the behaviors and attitudes of the mothers, these findings are consistent with what we'd assume intuitively. Moms who are especially attentive to their kids and address their needs one-on-one as valid human beings are more likely to bear secure attachment styles.

Avoidant and resistant styles, lumped together as being "insecure," seemed to arise from moms who were less sensitive to their children's needs—whether that was manifested through being openly impatient, incompetent when it came to attending to them, or neglecting them.

While it's regrettable that there is such a large contingent of mothers whose children are insecurely attached, it should come as at least a small comfort that many children studied were found to be securely attached—meaning despite the prevalence and existence of insecure attachment, at least it's not as common as being securely attached. Though we've only looked at moms and babies in a laboratory environment, we can extend this to our lives too—becoming more comfortable and trusting in our relationships can open us to the great benefits of intimacy, well past our "goo-goo, ga-ga" years.

HARLOW'S MONKEYS

If that last study didn't convince you of the necessity of love and warmth, maybe this one will. You might often hear, unfortunately, people who have had issues with their caregivers may feel bad about criticizing them. A common line that a down-on-themselves kid with troublesome caregivers might use when trying to defend them sounds like, "At least they gave me food, clothes, and shelter," as if providing basic necessities isn't the bare minimum owed to the child. If we're talking about bare necessities, though, and only include things like food and not genuine love, then are we being accurate? It may sound like a scientifically flimsy question, but one would not be faulted for asking: "What is more essential for a child's survival: food or love?"

At the time of the experiment we're about to talk about (so the mid-to-early-1900s), the debate was cold toward the notion that maternal love was "real." The "scientific" explanation for maternal bonding was that since the mom provided food to the newborn throughout all of our history as sapient beings, it stands to reason that the baby grows attached to the mom since she's the hub for nutrient acquisition and therefore survival. You can see echoes in this in animal training—you know how you try to gain an animal's trust usually by giving it something to eat first? Then it starts associating you with food providence and comes to like you, or so the theory goes. But what if this isn't the right way of looking at things? What if the order isn't "providing survival needs leads to love" but rather "providing love leads to survival"?

Psychologist Harry Harlow was perhaps inspired by this notion that there was more to a child's craving for love beyond it being a mechanism for telling their mother that they needed attention. In his now-famous experiment, he constructed two "mothers" for newborn baby rhesus monkeys—one made of soft, comfortable cloth great for hugging and one made of metal wire, which was uncomfortable to hug.

Much like the Strange Situation experiment, Harlow had the baby monkeys roam free in an unfamiliar environment with and without their mothers. Now you may be thinking, why would the monkeys ever go to the wire mother for anything? The cloth mother has soft hugs and warmth, so if the monkey needs to be comforted or coddled, it'd go to the cloth mother, right? Well, Harlow tried to level the playing field by giving the wire mother the distinct "advantage" of holding a baby bottle full of baby monkey food. It was now a choice between an unhuggable mom who provided sustenance and a soft, "affectionate" mom that could provide comfort and not much else.

They honestly looked a lot scarier than this in reality.

Shockingly, it turns out that the baby monkeys never hung out with the wire mother under any circumstances unless they were hungry. In the situation of being distressed because of a new environment, the monkeys chose the warm embrace of a mother utmost before thinking about survival needs. Of course, in versions of the trial where Harlow had the cloth mother hold the bottle and the wire mother hold nothing, there was no reason for the baby to go to the wire mother for anything. Regardless of what the mother could provide for the baby in terms of material things, the baby relied on her to feel safe and return to her while exploring the room as long as she had hugs waiting for them at the end of the day. At the cost of becoming a controversial figure in the discussion of psychology experiment ethics, Harlow had illustrated his point to the world: babies require nourishment for their hearts as much as they need nourishment for their bellies.

NATURE VERSUS NURTURE

"What is the formative element of destiny—
the beginning or middle?"

No matter how hard it tries not to be, a mouse is genetically locked in to be afraid of cats. Just as well—cats are genetically locked in to hunt mice. *C'est la vie!* But what if you super-trained a cat to be vegetarian and pet mice instead of eating them? Couldn't you technically do that with a strong punishment for hunting mice and a strong reward for petting mice? Anyone will tell you it's a lost cause—despite how ridiculously smart cats can sometimes be, they cannot betray their instincts. So many million years of genetics hard-coded them to one-shot mice on sight, and that can't change after some intense catnip bribing.

Not like us humans, though. The traditional definition of wisdom, or at least temperance, is the ability to resist the primal urge to do the wrong thing, even if it's the easy thing. No other known life form has the quality of "wisdom" like this—it's like we call the shots on what parts of our ancestral behavior come to the surface and what stays repressed. Despite the numerous examples this book provides of us not being able to override our neural circuitry, on a broader analysis we are decent at not giving in. We are great at learning and just as importantly, we're great at applying the things we learn. If someone gives you feedback, you usually take it into account for the next time you're in a similar situation.

But that capability, too, is inherently genetic, isn't it? The fact that we have human DNA is decidedly what makes us human, and if our DNA is the only difference between us and other animals, then that's got to be where our capability for plasticity comes from. That's not all though—DNA doesn't launch us on a blind voyage into the darkness to absorb whatever the people around us tell us, which becomes our personality. No, there must be a genetic component in the way every individual lives— anecdotally, you may see personality traits that run in your family or friends' families. You can attribute that to parenting styles and techniques being passed down through generations, but what about all those accounts of people who end up being exactly like their parents after being estranged or separated from them? What about how unrelated people end up so different from each other even if they are raised in similar conditions? This kind of stuff may seem too anecdotal to be a basis for scientific inquiry, but it's a huge point of debate in many domains of thought— philosophical, biological, and psychological included.

This debate is usually framed as the "nature versus nurture" debate—how much of someone's personality and life experience is determined by their genetics (i.e., their innate "nature") versus how they were raised and what was present in their environment (i.e., how they were "nurtured"). What's your opinion? Think about it for a second—and think about it carefully. How much can villains be blamed for their actions? Are their bad circumstances to blame? Can anyone be a star basketball player in an environment focused enough on making them into one? Is it genetic determinism? It might be a fun thought exercise to chew on as we delve into some studies that touch upon this subject.

THE BOBO DOLL EXPERIMENT

Once upon a time, a bossy crab and her son walked on the beach. The mother crab noticed that her son, scuttling behind her, was only walking sideways and couldn't see where he was going. She sighed and turned to reprimand him.

"Stop doing that! You'll trip and fall. Walk with one foot in front of the other, like a good boy!"

The little crab, taken aback, examined his feet before looking back to his mother and said, "I don't know how to walk like that. Can you show me?"

The mother hesitated before realizing she had never walked like that before and therefore did not know how to do it herself.

This is a famous fable but not famous enough that I thought everyone reading would know what I'm talking about if I just said, "Remember the mother crab story?" While the story isn't as famous as its contemporaries, like the tortoise and the hare, it *is* heavily associated with a well-known phrase: "Do as I say, not as I do."

The story is meant to clown on the phrase a little bit, both from a moral standpoint and a practical wisdom standpoint. How can you expect people to act according to a standard that you can't meet? How are you making it easier for them to quit bad habits if you can't lead by example? The story may have a lot more practical basis than we might give it credit for at first glance—at least, that's what psychologist Albert Bandura found from his Bobo doll experiment.

Bandura had a child play with toys in the same room as, but separately from, an adult who also had a few toys to play with—one of them being a Bobo doll. You know, the thing in the picture here. You can hit it and it will swing back toward you harmlessly. Or harmfully, if it has a spike or bomb attached to it.

Bandura would have some of the adults beat up the Bobo doll during their play session while others were assigned to ignore it. At the end of the joint play session, Bandura would aggravate the child by taunting them with new toys before taking them away. Yeah, that'll do it.

He then had the child play with a new set of toys, including the Bobo doll. And...yep, I think you can guess what happened. The children who witnessed the adult unleashing their hundred-hit combo of wrath on the Bobo doll were far more likely to vent their frustration of having their toys taken away by abusing the Bobo doll than children in the same room as a peaceful adult, who would rather cool off and play with the toys normally.

Bandura expanded the experiment further to get more specific on what it was about the aggression that was triggering the kids' wild sides, but the only thing that mattered was the presence of violence. It didn't matter if the violent one was a real person, cat, or cartoon, and it didn't matter if the violent person was seen being rewarded or punished for this behavior. The only thing that mattered was whether the violent person was the same gender as the kid—maybe it's like a role model or kinship thing.

MINNESOTA TWIN STUDY

If aggression gets left unchecked in a child's early life, they will be severely hampered for the rest of their life. Those first few bonds are crucial for keeping them up-to-speed with their peers in terms of development, and if they mess those up by being disproportionately selfish, violent, or withdrawn, it could spell a bad time for the kid in their future, even as adults. So let's try to make sure we don't beat up any Bobo dolls in front of impressionable children. Please promise me. There are better, more discreet ways to release anger. But if you beat up a thousand Bobo dolls, how much can it veer a kid off-course?

The Minnesota Twin Study of Twins Reared Apart (ostensibly "MTSTRA" for short, but no one calls it that because I made it up just now), conducted by psychologist Thomas J. Bouchard Jr. (what a great name!) was a study initiated in 1979 to take a closer look at how different your life and personality can get depending on the kind of life you have. Let's say you have an exact clone of yourself born at the exact same time as you—will your clone end up in jail while you are an upstanding citizen because your clone witnessed the brutal wombo combo-ing of a Bobo doll and you didn't?

Biologically speaking, twins/triplets/quadruplets/etc. are the closest thing you can get to separate people with nearly identical genetics. This means they're ideal subjects for investigating how much genetics determines our destiny versus how much environment determines it.

Since these twins have the same genes, the difference in their hat choices can't be chalked up to genetics and therefore must be environmental.

Bouchard was interested in how different twins could end up if they were raised apart versus in the same household. He put many twin pairs, both estranged and raised together, through tests to assess their similarities and differences in personality, interests, and IQ. It was the golden opportunity to find out if these sorts of things were determined by DNA, and if so, how much. It was finally time to answer the question burning in our minds: would a child raised by a stubborn crab only know how to walk sideways and strongly dislike seagulls?

The answer? Probably not. Regardless of if the twins were raised together or separately, their "similarity" was assessed to be somewhere around 50 percent. Dang, so that's a total knockout for the "nature" side of the "nature versus nurture" argument, right?

You should know at this point that whenever "right?" comes up in this book, it leads to some plot twist. Well, here it is, delivered on time: while we know there's a massive amount of heavy lifting done by genetics, nurture isn't completely down for the count. It could be genetics determine how sensitive we are to being influenced by certain things in the environment and what we pay attention to while growing up. Incidentally, this study also found that IQ is about 30 percent based on your environment (i.e., how you were raised), so the other 70 percent is essentially what you were born with. This may be somewhat baseless conjecture, but it could be that this gives a decent general figure for how much we are overall determined and influenced by our surroundings: 70 percent nature and 30 percent nurture. Figuring out specific details like that is for future twin studies to find out, maybe!

PLAYING NICE

"Does charity purely serve a tax function?"

"Prosocial behavior"—do you know what that is? "Pro," as in "encouraging," "social" as in "society," and then "behavior"—a behavior that encourages the betterment of society. We think of this in the context of altruistic action, such as giving to charity or paying your peer a compliment. Even more basic than this, you can also participate in prosocial behavior by just...not being a menace: obeying the law and obeying unwritten social rules (e.g., "don't interrupt others," "don't burp at a funeral," "don't smear an entire jar's worth of peanut butter all over the walls").

This section is interested in that first part, though—the proactive business of it all: volunteering, gift-giving, the whole shebang. If you, lovely reader, are particularly pessimistic about these concepts, it might be that you identify with the social exchange theory of prosocial behavior. The social exchange theory states we essentially do good things because it eventually comes back to reward us. Whether the reward structure looks something like "give to charity to not feel guilty," or "compliment someone's clothes to receive a compliment back," or "volunteer because it makes you look good," at the end of the day, it all comes back to benefit you. And hey, that's not necessarily a criticism—is it so bad that acting out of self-interest in this way produces nice results for everyone? It's all win-win, right?

This is what we might call an "egoistic view" of altruism, which is opposed to the "empathy-altruism hypothesis." This is the view that, while altruism happens to have these benefits baked into them, the origin of altruism is in its initial resolution of concern for your fellow human. When you don't have this emotional connection, the social exchange structure might kick in, but real altruism **does** exist! However, it's hard to carry this view openly without being called "foolishly idealistic" or "that weirdo who smears peanut butter all over the walls," and you'd bet that it was not any different back in the day either.

BATSON AND TRUE ALTRUISM

Daniel Batson, social psychologist, believed altruism was more than a convoluted way of enacting self-serving behavior. Enacting his earnest expedition of eliciting elucidations external to egoism,

Batson formulated a plan to capture moments of "true altruism" on paper to be immortalized in the scientific literature.

Batson had a group of psychology students observe what they thought was someone taking a ten-part memory test. In reality, as you may have guessed, it was an actress pretending to be doing the test. The story that the students were led to believe was that the woman's punishment for doing poorly on the test was to be given an electric shock (and they made sure to make it clear that the shocks hurt). After watching this uncomfortable situation for a while, the students were given an option: they could elect to take the electric shocks in the woman's place, or they could leave the scene early after only watching two of the ten trials. A different group of students was given a slightly different choice: take the shocks in her place or watch her finish the test, which included watching her endure the electricity punishments until the end of the experiment.

The students went with the "easier" choice in either situation. When given the option to peace out, they did so more often— while the students who would have been forced to watch the uncomfortable scene unfold chose to sacrifice themselves more often. The idea here is the discomfort of having to watch the electric shocks caused more trouble within the students' minds than the brief, physical discomfort of having to be shocked. On the other hand, those who had the option of leaving quickly and painlessly chose to do so because it was a no-trade-off way to avoid trouble.

Now here comes the hard part: is this true altruism? Maybe, right? Altruism being motivated by empathy and not personal gain was displayed here, right? The emotional pain of watching someone in pain was not worth direct, personal harm being inflicted on them—so this was a clear example of the human inclination to let empathy take precedence over survival, right?

Oh, there it is again, the "right?" of doom. Yeah, no. Proponents of social exchange theory might spin the results the opposite way; the tendency for people to get out of dodge if the opportunity was easy indicated that self-preservation was the priority for most people. Meanwhile, to explain the small portion of people that *did* take to choose the electric shocks, other things could've gone wrong for the participants if they chose otherwise—what if the woman came out of the room after the experiment and got mad at them? There could be untold social repercussions! Any way you slice it, the participants are trying to cut down their discomfort levels and that's got to be egoistic altruism.

Or is it?

There is a second part to this experiment—Batson conducted this under two conditions—one where the participants were convinced the woman was similar to them (thus eliciting high empathy) and one where the participants were convinced that the woman was dissimilar to them (the "low empathy" condition).

The results we discussed earlier were what happened in the low empathy condition, but in the high empathy condition, participants chose to take the electric shocks in her place consistently regardless of whether they had an easy way out. Remember, the hypothesis was not about whether people would choose to do the "nice" thing or how frequently it may happen—it was about where the motivation to do nice things came from, regardless of how often it happened. While the social exchange theory says it's a matter of balancing how beneficial being selfish versus being nice would be, the findings here say otherwise—it seems when we decide to do the nice thing, it's because we've determined it meets an empathy threshold rather than a discomfort threshold.

That's right; we pulled a double plot twist with the "right?" into the "or is it?" combo. In other news, we're open to accepting any former cynics onto our "belief in the beauty of the indomitable human spirit" boat.

LIKING PEOPLE AND LIKE-LIKING PEOPLE

"What do you like about me?"

Don't fret; this section is in fact not about video game monsters attracted to you because they want to eat your shield. We're dealing with a different breed of beast—earthling humans! In case it wasn't clear, everything mentioned in this book thus far only applies to Earth-native people; results for extraterrestrial beings are inconclusive. That raises the question though— what's up with the term "star-crossed lovers"? How pompous of us to assume the crossed-ness of our stars when we fall in love. Of course, it'd only be pompous if we didn't have any empirical evidence to back up the claim, but that's something we fortunately have. And we have a lot of it.

The literature on relationships (platonic, romantic, societal, or otherwise) is extensive. You've seen just as much—what with the Harlow monkeys, Bobo dolls, and the like. It's one of the most archaic human motivators in so many domains—that darn emotion of love has got to be responsible for at least half of all art ever created, if not more. That is not a researched figure; it's rhetorical. Please don't hit us with the fact-check smite of journalistic integrity doom. The point is, love is so always on our minds that we can't help but get curious about it, including in a scientific way. All stages and forms of love are of interest to us, as the breadth of research indicates we aren't picky—friendships, crushes, marriages, families, altruism—it's all part and parcel of human history. Now all that isn't to exclude people who can't have a lived experience of certain types of love due to personal dispositions or life conditions but is more so to outline the undeniable ubiquity of love in the public consciousness.

The sheer volume of work looking into love and relationships is far beyond the scope of one book, let alone one section of one chapter of one book. To prevent this section from becoming thicker than a bowl of oatmeal, we'll keep it brief and give a little crumb taste test sample of the science about relationships that seems kinda fun.[1]

GAIN-LOSS THEORY

Aw, come on; a theory about relationships that uses words like "gain" and "loss"? Didn't we spend that whole altruism section talking about how we can't evaluate abstract things like relationships based on calculations of cost versus benefit? Are we about to dip back into the idea that we are gaining and losing things from relationships and our brain interprets them as "connections"? Way to break the romantic illusion within one chapter, ya dingo!

First, a dingo is a smart dog-like animal. They are cute but I think public opinion on them is mixed. Don't quote me on that; as far as I know, they were once thought of as agricultural pests, but it's unknown if they're their own species and now they are close to being endangered or something.

Second, this is more like a "trick" phenomenon akin to the superfluous apology trick than an operationalized view of relationships. The gain-loss "trick" is simple: people tend to like you better if they think they grew on you over time versus if they think you liked them the same amount the entire time. Use that knowledge as you will.

---

1   Fun not guaranteed. Expect at your own risk. We are not responsible for any yawns, eye rolls, or premature page flips due to our selections.

This discovery arose after psychologists Elliot Aronson and Darwyn Linder set out to find if people put more emphasis on the journey rather than the destination when it came to friendship. Stay with us on this one, because it carries fascinating implications about things that aren't interpersonal relationships.

Aronson and Linder set up a few meetings between a volunteer participant (we'll call them "A") and an actor pretending to be another participant ("B"). During the meetings, the two were made to interact with each other before a brief intermission where A was led to believe they were eavesdropping on B talking to the experimenter about their opinion of A. There were four possible "stories" that played out at random through B's evaluations, which were as follows:

1. B started their first few assessments with a negative view of A before warming up to them, culminating in a final view that was positive.

2. B's assessments were all positive.

3. B's assessments started positive but gradually became more and more negative.

4. B's assessments were all negative.

As was spoiled earlier, A liked B the most when they could win them over, more than if B had a positive opinion the whole time. Interestingly, the opposite was true: A disliked B a lot if their opinion went from good to bad and disliked them for this more than if B disliked A the whole time.

Thinking about this a little deeper, this can come with a few interpretations. Perhaps the feeling of successfully convincing someone to like you is deeply meaningful, like a reward for putting in the effort of being likable. A's positive assessment of B, aside from being influenced by the good feeling of knowing someone genuinely thinks they're swell, may be from a generous perception that attributes good qualities to B post-hoc. "They are a good listener," "They are patient," "They are kind," etc.—it could be part of them that hopes B must be a good person to have found goodness in them.

Curiously, this could have meaningful applications in leadership and winning public opinion. For leaders, it may be a good technique to get your team to follow you more willingly if you give them a narrative of improvement to work with. Criticize and encourage them where they go wrong or fail to meet expectations but acknowledge where they are making improvements and show them that your opinion of them will go up when they do something well—it'll help them establish their growth story while earning you likability points in the meanwhile. Now whether this makes them improve is a different story. Even if it doesn't make them into the worker you wanted them to be, at least you know an easy way to make them more likely to buy you a cookie.

LOVE BRIDGE

Okay, yeah, that's cool; gain-loss, leadership, dingoes, whatever—what about the juicy stuff? Like, how do I get the cutie in the corner over there to fall head over heels in love with me? You got all these psychology tricks on how to get people to buy jam or how to get a monkey to ask you for milk, but I need a way to get that person to not run away screaming when I offer them a Valentine's Day card. I got you, friend—enter the love bridge.

I guess you can't enter a bridge; it's more like you step on it. You ever wonder why people recommend pretty places like aesthetic cafés or scenic parks for date locations? It's probably because subconsciously it works to some degree to make the person of interest start associating you with the beauty of the scenery. All you had to do was stand next to the landscape to get lumped in with how great it is. Cool! On the other hand, have you ever heard people recommend an amusement park or a horror movie as a first date idea? You might think those are awful ideas—nothing screams romance like hair getting messed up from a frantic and speedy roller coaster, right? How about the seductive mien of killer monsters chasing a bunch of screaming teenagers on the big screen? Yeah, I'll pass on those date ideas.

...is what a *fool* would say! Science says that those ideas might not be so counterproductive as you'd think—in fact, they could be counter-counterproductive. So...productive.

The wacko who suggested those dates probably learned a thing or two from psychologists Donald Dutton and Arthur Aron. (Remember him? I'll give you a hint: Chapter 4!) Dutton and Aron figured since the psychological state of arousal (when your awareness is heightened due to your body sensing it's time to take action) could be induced by both fear and having a crush on someone, it's possible that sometimes we mix up our feelings with our thoughts regarding what caused those butterflies. Think about it—if you are about to do something scary, it's the same feeling as when you are about to talk to someone you have a huge secret crush on. We often say that we get "scared" or "nervous" around someone we have a crush on when this feeling gets strong—while that's not inaccurate, it's also not exactly accurate—the psychological term is the catch-all term of "arousal."

Playing around with this theory, Dutton and Aron had an attractive female assistant approach random men while crossing a bridge and asked them to fill out a questionnaire. Afterward, they were given her number and asked to call her if they had any questions. The fun part about this experiment is that it was conducted on two bridges—one sturdy, non-scary bridge and one dangly, high, scary bridge. The men were more likely to call the number to talk to the assistant if they had encountered her on the scary bridge—which Dutton and Aron interpreted as misattributing their fear of the bridge to feeling butterflies for the assistant and therefore deciding they should call her. This "misattribution of arousal," as the experimenters dubbed it, tells us the lesson we've consistently heard since Chapter 1—that we may not be as in control of our thoughts as we believe.

It should be noted that this study is controversial. Some follow-ups have shown you can't "accidentally" interpret bad-feels as good-feels. This study is so famous that it wouldn't be a terribly unsafe bet to make that the controversiality of this study is the actual "cool, new fact" part of this section. But listen, don't tell me you wouldn't feel some sort of I'm-glad-I-made-it-out-of-that-alive endorphin-based comradeship with someone you go through something scary with. That scary rollercoaster or movie may have your crush feeling butterflies, and they may not be fooled into thinking that they're for you, but who knows—they could get so scared that they end up grabbing your hand! Scandalous!

CHAPTER 6

CHAOS IN THE MIND

ABNORMAL PSYCHOLOGY & UPSETTING SITUATIONS

You know it, I know it, we all know it: to varying degrees and for every reason in the world, life is hard. It just is. As we discussed at the beginning of this book, mental health is a real concern and it's something many, if not all, of us will have trouble with in some way or another at some point. Abnormal psychology is a pattern of activity marked by nonstandard behavior or thought patterns—you might know of some famous abnormal psych terms such as depression, anxiety, schizophrenia, psychosis, sociopathy, narcissism—the list goes on, but you get the picture.

Abnormal psychology often has a negative perception, and it's not a surprise—one of the fundamental human motivators, as we've discussed in several previous chapters, is to "fit in" or to "be like everyone else." By definition, having something that makes you different or abnormal would serve to distance yourself from that ideal situation. So is it a bad thing to have depression or anxiety or schizophrenia? Are we going to not fit in if we have any of these afflictions? Do we not have a place at all? Should we always aim to be like everyone else?

The general answer is—it depends. Being "normal" for the sake of being "normal" is not only a vague goal but can sometimes diminish the great things that make you unique. You should still aim to minimize your discomfort, so it's generally good to take steps to overcome what ails you (whatever "overcoming" may look like) if it is something genuinely able and recommended to be dealt with and you have the guidance and go-ahead of a professional.

Speaking of professionals, even though we've emphasized several times that this book is for fun and definitely no replacement for a therapist or doctor, it's especially relevant in *this* section that we double, triple, quadruple emphasize this—it is fantastic to be aware of the facts surrounding mental health, but it is not advisable to self-diagnose and it is *absolutely* super, ultra, omega not advisable to self-medicate. I just added "omega" to that, so that's how you know I mean it. If you have an issue and are hesitant to contact a professional, consult someone you trust to assist you in seeking help.

Having some things about you that are categorized as "abnormal" is not a reason to feel discouraged, ashamed, or like something is "wrong" with you. Though the perception of abnormal psych and the general connotation of the word "abnormal" might be overcast to most, the outlook doesn't have to be so dreary. Abnormal psychology also extends to things that aren't sad or need "fixing"; it's a categorization method that tells us something is a little different, not that anything is missing. But since we should always try to be understanding of other people to the level of the individual anyway, the fact that we're going to need to account for what makes them unique is a given no matter what. At the end of the day, we don't know what someone else is going through just by looking at them, so it's important to be considerate of others in general. With that out of the way, let's explore this fascinating aspect of the brain.

THE MIND WEIGHS AROUND THREE POUNDS

"Is a bad thought just a neurochemical impulse gone wrong?"

A mental illness is an illness all the same. When your tummy hurts, you seek treatment from a tummy doctor. When your mind hurts, you seek treatment from a mind doctor. You get what I mean? A crisis in the brain means you have a legit, sirens-blaring emergency going on in a real, squishy organ in your body—the one that weighs around three pounds on average and houses a bunch of neurons and serves as the command center in your head.

While we typically think of "malady of the brain" in an abstract sense, caused by intangible things like words, events, and thoughts, it's no secret that the brain is affected physically as well. You'd be quick to point fingers at hormones, neurotransmitters, and the like, with long-term exposure to some of them having lasting physical effects on the body. You can reason out, then, that the brain's function is impacted heavily by its physical condition, right? Things like mood disorders and aging eventually cause a reduction in the brain's gray matter, for example, which impairs critical functions like memory.

It's hard to separate the idea of impaired or irregular brain function from the world of the unseeable, considering we can't see someone's brain while observing them. It's like something that is above them, in a sense. Almost as if it's not their brain that is in peril but their soul. For example, there are numerous accounts of brain tumor patients suddenly having aggressive shifts in personality, mood, behavior, and attitudes before they're diagnosed. From the perspective of knowing that they had a physical disturbance in the region that handles thought, we have a more clinical grasp of the situation, but to the loved ones of those patients, it would have seemed more like a supernatural occurrence. Let's step back and attempt to tap into our ability to assess the brain as what it physically is—an organ.

THE CURIOUS CASE
OF PHINEAS GAGE

Phineas Gage was a railroad worker who had a name evocative of the time in which he lived—the mid-1800s. Like, seriously, you probably knew right away that this study happened a long time ago when the main character of it has a name like that. It's one of those wise-sounding names that you'd find in a storybook belonging to a detective or a wizard. But getting back to real-world Phineas Gage, he had had the misfortune of suffering an accident where his head was severely injured by taking an iron rod to the skull. In consideration for you, lovely reader, I will be light on the exact details of the injury in case you're squeamish. Point is, he survived and was treated but began to show changes in personality and behavior.

Doctor James Martyn Harlow (no relation to the guy who did the monkey experiment in Chapter 5) was the physician attending to Gage and observed these changes in real-time. Understand— these were 1800s times. This all went down several years before

Sigmund Freud was born, nearly two decades before Canada had become a country, and about a decade before toilet paper was invented, if that gives you an idea of how long ago that is. The literature on neuroscience wasn't as prolific or elaborated as it is today, and we still had a lot of kinks to work out in the models of what "thought" is.

The 1800s

| NAPOLEON IS DEFEATED | PHINEAS GAGE GETS INJURED | TOILET PAPER IS INVENTED |

As somewhat expected, Gage had physical impairments after his incident—vision problems, partial paralysis, and difficulty with coordination, to name a few. Gage also suffered from seizures and a loss of his sense of smell. These seemingly distant functions were all caused by the same injury—which was quite a curious idea at the time. What was not as expected were Gage's emotional and cognitive shifts—he seemed incapable of certain higher functions such as coordinating plans and making decisions. Social stimuli that may have previously been picked up on pre-injury now flew over Gage's head, and he could not control himself emotionally. Ultimately, Gage could not hold down a job and lived the rest of his years dependent on his family. His mental state deteriorated more and more, with increasingly frequent seizures marking the months leading up to his death.

Dr. Harlow's case study of Phineas Gage endures today as a breakthrough in understanding how the physical object of the brain is complexly intertwined with concepts as nebulous as behavior, personality, and cognition. Lots of subsequent research leapfrogged off of Harlow's work and generally credits it as one of the foundational episodes that established the link between brain and being.

STEPPING OUT BRAVELY

"How much worse are we making it for ourselves?"

Labels are important. Areas in which this is applicable are kitchens, chemistry labs, and offices, to name a few. If you know what category something belongs to, you'll know when and how to deal with it. The label of "nut" in the kitchen, for instance, lets us know we shouldn't have to access that entire category of things if we're preparing a dish for someone with a peanut allergy. If a small fire breaks out in a chemistry lab, you can automatically eliminate anything labeled "non-flammable" as having been part of the problem. People are kind of the same with their labels, as we saw when we discussed identity and groups. This also applies to things like diagnoses—you'll often see people are relieved to hear the name of their illness when they see a doctor, even if the condition is bad. This is because knowing the name of the disease and thus beginning a plan to treat it is better than knowing you have some unidentified illness without knowing what will make it better or worse.

The truth sets us free, in a way. It gives us a good picture of the situation that we can operate within. Even if the conditions aren't ideal, at least they're in view. If smaller doses of perspective can improve our lives like this, then as people with a vested interest in reducing suffering, we could then ask: what are the limits of this? Just how essential is the truth for the pursuit of mental wellness?

TERROR MANAGEMENT THEORY

Have you ever heard of the phrase, "Going mad at the revelation"? Maybe someone finds out that their favorite band doesn't make any of their own music and they start freaking out and having what kind of looks like an identity crisis. One of the most universal "truths" that disturbs people to their core is the reality that we will all die someday. When it's a distant, scientific fact, it's usually okay to deal with, but thinking about it for too long and in too much detail is asking for a freak-out to happen. Don't do it right now! Don't freak yourself out! You have a book to read, after all.

Being as old and prevalent a problem as it is, one has to wonder if human awareness of mortality has any quick-fix defense mechanisms that help us deal with it. To explore that, social psychologists Jeff Greenberg, Sheldon Solomon, and Tom Pyszczynski developed the terror management theory (TMT). In 1986, the trio set off to produce an experimental finding that would prove that fear of death influences our actions by setting up an experiment where participants would write down their thoughts and feelings about their own deaths. Lovely. They also had a separate group of participants who did the same thing, but instead of writing about death, they wrote about some random, non-death thing.

After this was done, the participants were presented with controversial topics such as censorship or religion and subsequently asked to give a personal approval rating of someone who would agree with them on these topics and a separate rating for someone who would disagree with them. Can you try to guess what happened in each group? Maybe you can guess, but can you guess why this happened?

Well, hope you took some time to think about it because the result is about to be spoiled for you forever (unless you forget): people who were reminded of their mortality were more likely to give more negative evaluations to people who disagreed with them. The idea is that being reminded of the fragility of our tether to the corporeal world made people more defensive and adamant about their worldviews. That's a rather arbitrary result to take in at first—of all the ways we choose to freak out, we do it by...getting political?

It's a case of the feet still pedaling long after the bike is gone. Part of TMT says the initial defense we set up against existential terror is establishing a sense of purpose. This sense is derived from establishing things that are important to us, like who we choose to care about and what we choose to be interested in, and eventually extends to general political opinions and attitudes. If you get your sense of purpose from being a good friend to the people around you, for example, then you may value friendship, inclusivity, and generosity. This allocation of values can, in turn, inform your political opinions on things like global affairs and welfare programs.

When the base issue of your mortality is disturbed, it plucks at the strings of your terror management structures and calls for emergency intervention from your sense of purpose so it can protect you from that terror. Now that your sense of purpose is on high alert, so are the associated attitudes and beliefs. This could be why people seem more unwilling to change their attitudes the older they get.

From a science standpoint, it wouldn't be difficult to imagine that vividly pondering the fact that you will die someday would set off some alarms in your body—it doesn't know much better, after all. "What's this sudden heightened concentration of thoughts about my death? Are my death-related brain circuits firing because I'm about to die? Activate the self-defense protocol!"—your brain and body are stuck in caveman times regarding things like this, unfortunately. Great for keeping our stone-age ancestors on their toes against unseen predatorial and environmental threats to their lives, not so great at keeping us cool and collected while running death simulations in our heads in the living room. We could go on and on about TMT; it's terrifyingly fascinating. Many concepts plug into it, and it's only being developed more and more by the day.

TOXIC CONNECTIONS

"Why do some people get away with hurting others?"

Major brain injuries and the inexorable march of death are big hitters in the league of disturbing things. No doubt, significant distress comes from all sources, but perhaps one of the most prevalent causes of grief is other people. Other people can be great—they can be fun, friendly, exciting, kind, and useful—but they can also be quite the doo-doo stain on our day—whether it's a bully, a narcissistic acquaintance, or someone who is excessively hostile or cruel.

Why do toxic friendships, toxic relationships, toxic families occur? Why are we cursed to care so much? What's going on in these people's heads? How bad would it be if left unchecked? The usage of the word "toxic" is more to settle you, lovely reader, into a framework to get ready to think about the general domain of people we're talking about since it's an easy, colloquial catch-all to describe upsetting or unpleasant people or phenomena, but overuse of the word in some circles has diluted its meaning. We won't keep using the term but know we're talking about *those* kinds of people. You know…you know.

The sheer scope of unhealthy relationships is so wide, deep, and varied that we couldn't ever hope to cover everything within a reasonable time. This stuff takes a lifetime of trial and error to learn, after all. Though with the number of pages this book has left means I can't exactly engorge you with the Library of Alexandria of toxic relationship experiments, what we can do is tickle your curiosity enough to whet your palate about the world of dysfunctional interaction research. Maybe with that spark of inspiration, you will be further motivated to explore the world of psychology on your lonesome! Speaking of lonesome, I'll leave you with one that is universally relevant along with a little explanation of what these mean people are doing to our brain chemistry.

OSTRACISM EXPERIMENTS

Is bullying all in your head? Does getting picked on cause you to feel a strong negative mood, or is there more going on in the mind when we feel like we're getting singled out? Like in terms of observable psychological phenomena that extend past "I feel bad."

"Ostracism" refers to being socially excluded, and you may not know but people don't like feeling excluded. While the science is clear about this, it's still interesting to see what is going on in the ol' noggin when we feel like people are rejecting us. It may be less painful if we were a loner from the beginning, but being in a situation where we feel we can fit in only to be left out can make us feel like we lost something we never had. It's like an extended version of the gain-loss theory.

Jean M. Twenge, Kathleen R. Catanese, and Roy F. Baumeister (this is his second appearance in the book!) wanted to find out the specifics behind the defense mechanisms we put up when we feel socially outcast. Their findings on the extent of the distress caused by ostracism were frightening—what was occurring in people who were upset at being rejected was called "cognitive deconstruction." We'll get back to cognitive deconstruction, but just know that it's what it sounds like—everything in the brain implodes and things like practical wisdom, cognitive capabilities, and emotions become impaired or suppressed.

The researchers conducted several experiments, so we'll go over them in sequence. One type of experiment involved having groups of participants come together to engage in an interactive activity for a few minutes before being brought aside and asked who they wanted to do part two of the experiment with. The experimenters then secretly disregarded their desires and grouped them off randomly, leaving one participant alone and told them no one in the group chose them for part two so they'd have to suck up the circumstances and continue.

Part two of the experiment was used to evaluate the differences between the grouped-up participants and the excluded participant, and across several experiments it was found that the excluded participant behaved strangely. They had slower reaction times, distorted time perception, and repressed emotions. Stay tuned to find out why.

The other experiment was where the participants were given a personality test that wasn't actually a personality test—the results were randomly distributed, and some of them received a result that told them they would likely end up alone later in life. Imagine a scientist handing you a personality test result that said you are destined to be alone—that's got to mess with you. Though the participants weren't likely to fully believe in the test's results, they still also had slower reaction times and were highly likely to sit away from mirrors when given a choice.

While the participants in these experiments were explicitly told they were excluded, other research on ostracization has shown that we're so sensitive to rejection that we can immediately feel like we're being excluded and start feeling the negative effects of it as soon as the suspicion arises. So, if you and your friends ever have an issue with someone, talk it out and compromise with them clearly and respectfully instead of ditching them. You might spare them the pain of cognitive deconstruction. Oh yeah, I said I'd get back to that, right?

COGNITIVE DECONSTRUCTION

What's the scoop on cognitive deconstruction? It's important to note this isn't exclusively caused by ostracization, but since being ostracized is a fundamentally impactful human tragedy, it's an effective way to induce it. To someone feeling rejected, the thought of reflecting on their ostracization is too painful, as they do not want to come face to face with and accept a part of themselves might be undesirable. This causes a systematic shutdown of anything that could delve into that area, which unfortunately doesn't leave a lot remaining.

Emotions are shut down to save oneself from acute emotional crises, leading to numbness. Anything that draws attention to self, like looking at mirrors, is limited. Since thinking about the implications and fallout of being ostracized could lead to revealing painful "truths" (even if these truths are emotionally exaggerated to be more upsetting than they realistically would be), the entire section of the mind that thinks about the future has been shut down as a defense mechanism against those painful simulations. This leads to ostracized individuals acting impulsively, leaving them unable to formulate thoughts about the future. When asked to generate a list of random words, for example, people going through cognitive deconstruction are far less likely to give future-tense verbs as an answer. Time goes slower. In an effect described as the opposite of "flow," cognitive destruction makes people so uninvested in meaningful activity and thought that every moment is painstakingly experienced in real time.

As you can see, this rundown of cognitive deconstruction might shed some light on why the rejected individuals in the ostracism experiments behaved how they did. The sad and perhaps scary part was they weren't aware that they were influenced by ostracism effects—it's not like they formulated a revenge plan against the group that abandoned them and had an elaborated life philosophy ready to adapt to their new, ostracized life. It just...happened.

It's important to recognize while it is truly awful to be the victim of someone else's wrongdoings, they are human just like us. That isn't to say they should be forgiven and given a pass; it means you are the same species as them and could've been the one doing the hurting if a few conditions were tweaked. That's not meant as a personal attack—it's more like, we need to make sure that we're solid enough in our morals that if we ever come across the same temptation that may have possessed the people who hurt us, we will still do the right thing. The complexity of human behavior is such that it's hard to tell if we're accidentally hurting someone without knowing it. It's hard to divide the world into victims and perpetrators with no overlap, because if you look deep down, it's not abundantly obvious that you're all that incapable of harm. But that's okay—maybe the reason that sometimes the bad guy gets to walk off whistling into the sunset as if nothing happened is because, quite often, that bad guy is us.

HOPE

"What's the point?"

What a world we live in. We're out here getting stressed and distracted by things out of our control, whipped up in the whirlwind of our genetic determinism, subject to the pressure of conforming to the crowd, and we can't be sure if what we're seeing is what we're seeing. How can we hold on to the aspiration of making anything of ourselves when the odds seem so stacked against us? Can we do it? Can we achieve the thing? You know, whatever "the thing" is to you. That purpose that keeps you pushing against existential dread. The feeling of almost reaching your goal only to fall short by a hair is sure to be crushing—and let's not think about falling short when you're far away from the goal.

That's a super tempting attitude to fall into. For starters, it absolves us of the responsibility of making things better. And it's true; there's a lot we might not be able to fight against due to the limitations of our body, including the silly little three-pound organ we keep in our skull. But our limitations are also what make us great! Right? Things can only be incredible and impressive if they have confines. Even something like nature, which we may think of as effortless and infinite, can be appreciated because it all happens under the strict rules of the universe. In us humans, the capacity to imagine a limitless potential and strive toward it despite everything must be worth something.

We have a word for pursuing a better tomorrow, and it's one of the most powerful ones we've got: "hope." Thus far, I've been speaking mostly in platitudes, so if that's not your cup of tea for being convinced, I'm pleased to present you with one last study that backs up the value of never giving up.

Biologist Dr. Curt Richter, famous for his research into the circadian rhythm, was experimenting on rats one day, as one does, when he noticed something strange. Being a man of his time, in classic, morbid 1950s fashion, Richter dropped rats into jars of water to see how long they would fight to survive. While nearly every single one of his rats died within minutes, he observed that several survived for a long time (like, sixty hours) before finally giving up.

Being a man of science foremostly, Richter skipped the rat eulogies and immediately shifted his interest to find the factors contributing to the rats' extraordinary survival capabilities. The conundrum was as follows: if all the rats can be assumed to want to survive through harsh conditions as much as the next, then why can some exhibit seemingly impossible capabilities in toughing it out while others succumb?

Richter was no idealistic romantic—he was not interested in the philosophical aspect of this ability, and he was not about to chalk it up to something unquantifiable like divine intervention or certain rats being "built differently." No, he would get to the biological basis of this phenomenon. What was the missing variable?

Richter took inspiration from real-life accounts of people dying from being "cursed." These people, being told that they could not escape the inevitable death curse cast upon them, stressed themselves into dying nearly instantaneously. Likening this to the situation with the rats, he surmised the rats were stressing themselves into a self-fulfilling death prophecy. With this hypothesis in mind, Richter engaged in his ethically dubious rat-dunking once more, only this time, he noted the state of the rats' hearts when they drowned. He noticed that instead of their hearts speeding up before drowning (which would indicate stress) they were slowing down, which indicated that the rats were essentially giving up and choosing to drown because they had lost hope for survival. Keep in mind since these are rats, they don't have a philosophy of "painless death"—they surely would've done anything to survive, but their bodies shut off in response to losing hope.

Curious about this new "hope" variable, he ran the experiment again, but this time, saving the rat from the depths when they were a minute or so from drowning. The rescued rat, though shaken, returned to normal after a short time. He then put the rat back into the situation, where the same remarkable survival abilities were shown once again. The simple addition of hope, a reason to keep going, was enough to make them go from drowning in minutes to swimming intrepidly for several days.

So how's that for hope? You are bursting with the potential to do so many great things, and the world is all the better. The best part is, everyone else also possesses this same potential for amazingness—so imagine the world we could build if we all did our part to take that potential and run with it as far as we can. Through the twists and turns that life presents, many of which cannot be avoided, we'd find our way, no doubt. We're not rats; we're much bigger and more capable! If a rat can find a reason to keep swimming beyond its reasonable limits, we can find it within us to keep swimming further than the mind's eye can see.